PORTRAIT OF JACQUES DERRIDA AS A YOUNG JEWISH SAINT

*European Perspectives*

# PORTRAIT OF JACQUES DERRIDA

# HÉLÈNE CIXOUS

*Translated by Beverley Bie Brahic*

# AS A YOUNG JEWISH SAINT

*Columbia University Press    New York*

Columbia University Press
*Publishers Since 1893*
New York   Chichester, West Sussex

Copyright © 2004 Columbia University Press
*Portrait de Jacques Derrida en Jeune Saint Juif* © 2001 Editions Galilée
Excerpts from Geoffrey Bennington's translation "Circumfession" in
*Jacques Derrida* (Chicago: University of Chicago Press, 1992) are reprinted by permission.

Columbia University Press wishes to express its appreciation for assistance given by the
government of France through the Ministère de la Culture in the preparation of this translation.

Library of Congress Cataloging-in-Publication Data
Cixous, Hélène
[Portrait de Jacques Derrida en jeune saint juif. English]
Portrait of Jacques Derrida as a young Jewish saint / Hélène Cixous ;
translated by Beverley Bie Brahic.
p. cm. — (European perspectives)
Includes bibliographical references.
ISBN–231–12824–X (alk. paper)
1. Derrida, Jacques—Religion. 2. Jews—Identity. I. Title II. Series
B2430.D484C5913 2003
194—dc22        2003055415

∞

Columbia University Press books are printed on permanent and durable acid-free paper.
Printed in the United States of America


c 10 9 8 7 6 5 4 3 2 1

# CONTENTS

AUTHOR'S NOTE    VII

A NOTE ON THE TEXT    XI

I. THE MARK OF THE PRINCE    I

II. NAMESAKES—NO! NO'S BY THE BUCKETFUL    3

III. OF THE KLEINS AND THE GROSSES    17

IV. THE DREAM OF NAÏVETÉ    29

V. REMAIN/THE CHILD THAT I AM    51

VI. POINT OF HONOR/POINT DONOR    63

VII. CIRCUMFICTIONS OF A CIRCUMCISION OBJECTOR    67

VIII. THE ORCHARD AND THE FISHERY    89

IX. SECOND SKIN    III

NOTES    125

WORKS CITED    135

## AUTHOR'S NOTE

You will of course have guessed that this portrait is to be somewhat unorthodox. UnCatholic in other words. What is a Young Jewish Saint [*Saint Juif*]? Given that its subject is Jacques Derrida, the inventor of *différance*, the poet who makes writing and hearing—and what an extraordinary sense of hearing he has—pair up and dance, this portrait is sotto voce and homophonically—do you hear?—that of a young *sainjuif*, I mean a Jewish monkey [*singe juif*], if there is such a thing, and why shouldn't there be a saintly monkey or a monkey of a saint?

And you are correct if, by paronomasia, you thought you saw the lightning silhouette of Saint-Just, figure of revolutionary exactitude, signifier (of the) rebel against all bounds and limits, slip in among the saints in *Je*.

But it all began, so they say, in 1930 with a J, with Jew, the word *juif* in French, at the heart of the French language.

What does "Jew" mean? Who can say "I am Jewish," without a shudder of the tongue and mind? Oh! this sentence and this verb *to be* in the present, always in the present, they demand reflection.

I have tried to portray him—the young Jacques Derrida—as he would like to be seen, in the tradition of Montaigne and later Rousseau, "according to my condition of female monkey" and, as the first would say, as "naked" as possible and also "in full" stark naked and hairy, neither covered nor uncovered but impelled by a *dream of impossible naïveté*, a desire to remain "in the raw" or "crude" he would say, in *Circumfession*.

It all almost didn't begin on July 15, 1930, the day his mother ought to have been expecting him, her poker day, a game the expectant woman could hardly interrupt without "being the loser" and that the child had to cut in on "at the last moment." Enter, between two fateful hands of poker: 1. a mother, a saint for not being one, and a queen with the sublime name of Esther, of whom he proclaims himself the remains; 2. the famous paradoxical logic that makes the philosophical heart of he who calls himself "the only replacement" beat, namely, *don, gagner à perdre, survivre, donner la mort* (gift, win by losing, survive, giving death) . . .

He is born between two deaths. Between two dead sons-of-the-mother. He is (born), he exists only between two deaths. Literature—that he is—lives on in place of the son of Esther-Amnesia.

But how to paint or sketch such a genius at substitution? At least in a single portrait? One must, one can only catch him, portray him in flight, live, even as he slips away from us. In these sketches we shall catch glimpses of the book's young hero rushing past from East to West, or from one shore to the other, in appearance both familiar and mythical: here he is for a start sporting the cap of Jackie Derrida Koogan, as *Kid*, I translate: lamb-child, the sacrificed, the Jewish baby destined to the renowned Circumcision scene. They steal his foreskin for the wedding with God, in those days he was too young to sign, he could only bleed. This is the origin of the immense theme that runs through his work, behind the words *signature, countersignature, breast* [*sein*], *seing* (contract signed but not countersigned), *saint—cutting, stitching—indecisions* . . . Let us continue.

Next he turns up in a turban, as Ali-Baba, alias Elie-Baba, no longer merely robbed but robber thief perjurer and re-robber *par jarres*, by the jarful. I meet up with him again later between a girl and a bunch of grapes, pulling the impish face of Cherubino the ribbon thief and all dolled up—in Suzanne's beribboned bonnet. The list never ends. Each comic opportunity reactivates the motif of the original theft, that of the scrap of round pink ribbon, the foreskin whose loss he has never been able to accept. What coif can take the place of that crown?

*Was I Jewish?* the fugitive muses. Will I ever have a chance to answer for "myself"? Who what me myself? Attached-detached-re-attached the undoer, the unreader par excellence, scoffer at borders, dry-witted prince, he pursues his infinite work that pursues him *passing (through) French* en *passant*.

A poet born-condemned, condemned to be *ifnotJewish*—hence the greatest philosophical player one can ever read. Read, un-read [*délire*], forget-read [*oub-lire*] and all that, let us recall it to the ear and not just to the eye.

No one has performed more learned yet more innocent pirouettes around words, no one has ever managed to get French stodginess more joyously drunk, giving philosophy the full measure of its greatness once and for all, which is both its tragic and its comic dimension. He makes writing laugh [*écrire*]. One cannot read him without being appalled at the urge to laugh—with enchantment.

"Was I happy? No, I had a taste of pleasure" Rousseau lamented, made "happy" despite himself. And he, Jacques Derrida, emulating that other genial monkey, could fret in turn: "Was I Jewish? No, I had a taste of pleasure." Never will he renounce any kind of taste, not happiness nor unhappiness either.

If *I weren't "Jewish,"* I tell myself, I wonder how, with what reticence, I should dare to speak of *it*, of this original wound, this ghostly dolor and of the Circumfiction that ensues. But *if I were Jewish* I tell myself, it would be even more daunting. But what does *Jew* mean, in a woman or man? This word, which traverses his entire life and mine, all his works and now this book, if we tried to gather up whatever trembles in its letters, there would be volumes and tomes to write. Let's cut it short:

The word *juif* is a French word, it is by means of French that I shall flit past in its pursuit, thanks to my initial subterfuge: I at least am not a "Jew" (masculine), either it's better or better it's worse, read on.

If we don't have circumcision in common, Jacques Derrida and I—at least that of the penis—the Circumcision to which Jacques Derrida has given its letters patent of noblewound, we have in common a number of precise and dated stigmata: Algeria 1940. But Circumcision and he are inseparable. Inseparable he is, and writes, from his own inaugural separation. Or is it *insepharable?*

# A NOTE ON THE TEXT

In the French *Portrait de Jacques Derrida en Jeune Saint Juif* the excerpts from Jacques Derrida's "Circumfession" were inserted into the relevant chapter. Periods 16, 10, and 17 were in chapter 2, period 8 was in chapter 3, period 1 was in chapter 4, periods 18 and 14 were in chapter 7, and periods 31 and 47 were in chapter 8. In English these excerpts have been grouped together in the middle of the book, where the reader may wish to refer to them to compare Hélène Cixous's marking of the French text of "Circumfession" with her analysis of the text.

PORTRAIT OF JACQUES DERRIDA AS A YOUNG JEWISH SAINT

# I

## THE MARK OF THE PRINCE

*Was I Jewish, he will have wondered all his life. Shall I have been Jewish? He is the prince of the interrogation mark, the prince on his mark, on the dot, on the point of being—of being Jewish, had there been ten mattresses stacked on his bed, and under the tenth, a tiny point no bigger than a needle's eye but whose point as piercing, as sharp, a bit of stitchery, he would still feel the pain what am I saying the mere idea of points is enough to give him a stitch in the side.*

*There is always a point in his vicinity, a bird as Kafka would say in search of its cage but not to shut itself in, to make it feel its caginess along with its liberty, I mean the all-inclusive potentiality but therefore also agape with limits bars partitions closures, the enclosure and the liberty of each and everyone, their sexual differences, there is always a dot, a point over here, an i somewhere else, I ought to join them and say a ni a neither, yes, a nid a nest, a bird's nest of signifiers of silkworms of hedgehogs, a secret nest, there is always a secretness secreting unprecedented liaisons, misdemeanors of delight or delirium, unraveling readings.*

*He is the dry-witted prince of the Jews, the scoffer, the mocker, what a word that is! the heart-word the word of words at the heart of the matter, the Derrider of eloquence and all its eloquence, a man of his word a man of heart, last analyst of the heart's aching, of the soul's suffering, did I say man I mean woman too, heart and soul, one is the laughter of the other, the smiling through tears.*

Here, a page into my first words you will already have understood that I can only portray him as a Jew in French, in all the French sleights of word, in this tongue, which he says is his sole language and that he does not possess, I mean does not have: on the one hand he can't bear the sight of it, or her, as we say in French, on the other hand he adores her, his whole life he has dreamed of having her, his Beauty

# II

## NAMESAKES—NO! NO'S BY THE BUCKETFUL

This is a story that begins with J. It was the fifteenth of July 1930.

It's about J; it's about a consonant still a little vowelish, a little i-ish in the aftermath of a magic philology.

Were I not "Jewish," I say to myself, holding the word to my lips shyly, in and with respect, were I unable to address this word to myself in some way, hesitatingly, with perplexity and in quotation marks, had I not from the age of three, in the throes of a world war, when I first began to trace the letters of the alphabet, unthinkingly signed a pact with the letter J among all the letters of the French language, the J, pronounced gee gît j'y, for Jew in my mother's secret wartime language: he's a J she would say, to say it without saying it, J the name of the secret, had J not been the name of the most French of all possible letters in the mouth of my German mother—for in German J does not gee, does not jeer, the J winks and wets, it's a yeu, yes, a *Jod*, pronounced *yod*, for me J was the alpha and omega of letters, the countersignature in person, the first person, if the first person in French, the personal pronoun, had not begun, clever letter, by the letter once damned and denigrated, had I not delighted in J from the very origins of my culture, I wonder how, with what audacity what timidity, I should dare to speak of *it*, this phantom pain—this sting, this morsel of remorse, this mental nibbling of the sex, of the heart, this male inauguration of memory by a bite mark—this primo-ablation of the cock's comb, this de-coronation, this prenatal toss of the dice, later vital and then already posthumous and after, but *if I were Jewish* I say to myself it would be even more daunting, but what does it mean Jewess? And Jew?

This word will have traversed his entire life and mine rousing such heavy seas. If he, if I, if we, born of parents all said-to-be-Jews, with our feeling for language, tried to fathom what takes place what resonates what raves vibrates, trembles for us in the word *Jew* and its letters, what a word! What this word represents, with its long history, with everything that everyone can say about it and beyond what everyone can say, volumes and tomes would have to be written, I shan't do that here. Between Jew, the word, and him as between the two invisible ends of an invisible cord run all the tremors of thought. It is a story of wit of words good and bad that I am going to tell, a story of reactions, of nervous responses, nervously poetic and philosophical, not a "Jewish joke of a story" (the only case where *Jew* has a place) but a story that is Jewish from the start and speaks of Jewish *in French.*

The word *juif* is a French word, it is in French that I shall slip past you in its pursuit like a madwoman fleeing, thanks to my initial subterfuge: I at least am not a Jew, either it's better or better it's worse, we shall see.

But through this word and without saying it we came to meet once, on the mountain, yes on a mountain as, one morning in the German language, Celan tells us in his admirable *Gespräch im Gebirg*, the Jew Gross came to Klein the Jew, and, says Celan, Klein, the Jew, bade his stick be silent in front of the Jew Gross's stick. At the foot of the Montagne Sainte-Geneviève, at the corner of the Rue St. Jacques and the year 1963, we came to the meeting as former children of said-to-be-Jews-born-in-Algeria whose book of memories had been inaugurated by similar events, events of war. And in this case Gross is him, Derrida, and Klein is me, and in those days I bade my stick be silent in front of his stick. Having been wounded by the same wounds, stung by the same bites, excluded by the same laws, mystified by the same bitter mystiflictions in Hebrew, struck with wonder as well at the same immense unique superJew figures, having followed, from a great distance, this or that Abraham's way of keeping one giant step ahead of disaster, many occasions, all of them cruel, unfolded between us their fragile silk impression of comprehension.

If we don't have circumcision in common (here I shall cease to call it by other names)—at least that of the penis, for the other that of the heart, I too have known—*the* Circumcision to which Jacques Derrida has given its letters patent of noblewound, we do mirror a number of precise stigmata, dated Algiers 1867, 1870, Oran 1940, 1942, 1954, 1956, all those dates of passovers, transfers, expulsions, naturalizations, de-citizenships, exinclusions, blacklistings, doors slammed in your face, dates of wars, of colonization, incorporation, assimilation, assimulation, indigene/ni/zations that constitute the archives of what he calls "my nostalgeria" and that I call my "algeriance," dates and plaques, my doctor father's nameplate yanked off the wall by Vichy, the psychic rash of plaques at the evocation of nationalist-racist outbreaks, tremors and symptoms at the portals of Schools.

So, in the Café Balzar, to rhyme with hazard, what did Gross and Klein find to talk of? Of exile and Joyce of phantasmic and literary Judaism, of the Jewflight of passages and of such very tame follies as being a foreigner-in-my-own-country, of circumconniving in the languages of translinguistic sport, of philosophical transports. Already of the Art of Replacement. "And only of letters, writing and literature," he reports, I quote from his memory, in "*H.C. pour la vie, c'est à dire.*"

The quoting had commenced.

"Before that, she has since told me," I quote, "many long years before that, some seven years before, she had seen and heard me—but from behind.

She had seen and heard me, from behind, speaking. Addressing the members of an academic jury, lecturing on the subject of death" (ibid).

I quote him, quoting me, quoting, dozens of years later, a trial scene at which I was present by chance, he and I facing the jury whose approval was needed to confer a degree, *the agrégation*, me facing his back, him with his back to me talking about death, already the subject of his thoughts. It was my first dose of Derrida.

He set the tone. All unawares, as a gift is given. I must have begun to make notes. This primal scene is a book in itself. I was with him in a foreign country, subject to the same *Passat* as Celan sings it, confronting the danger of an *agrégation*, but he wasn't with me, and for good reason. One "some" seven years later Gross und Klein at the Balzar what can they be talking of save the tone, the gift, the dose, of words forever foreign in the place they belong, of the true-false Jew Bloom put in circulation, in simulation, in Dyoubelong the uninhabitable Joycian Dublin, doubling for Paris. He speaks face to face as from in back, of life and death, of separation as inseparable, of himself, I thought, I believe, or maybe I felt, he speaks like an incurable wound. It was a book. The book of books.

"It's *as if*"—I quote him—"we had *practically* [*quasiment*] never been apart." I quote him exactly. This *as if* [*comme si*], his signature, his side step, never to abandon us, slipping its stylet, the tip of its *as-ifness* into the-not-be-apart, it is that of his Circumcision—his circumasifision, he was to call it.

But *the* Cir-concision, she with him, he and it are inseparable, and for all eternity in every reading. Inseparable he is from his own inaugural separation. Or is it *insepharable*? From this event, which has happened *but once apparently* within his life, as he is at pains to stipulate at the beginning of *Schibboleth,* and an incalculable number of times thereafter, all shall we say, without appearance, he has spun an infinite web, all of whose figures we shall not manage in our lifetime to perceive.

Innumerable is the opera of the Circumcision and yet yes in it we have a masterpiece of *concision*. To be brief: he writes concise. This concision, which gives his voice its force, can only be fully effective in French: it uses all the idiomatic resources of the language with which he has an ongoing (as he explains to the point of making a joke of it in *Le Monolinguisme*) and furious dispute, jealous as a tiger as he is of his verbal treasures, his means and his mines, I mean his galleries, his veins, his tropes, his figures, his facets, his feints, his perches for books. He says a thing. It is an appearance. The appearance covers and broods. Every sentence surpasses itself, in all directions, in every sense of the word. He himself can't keep up, it's the fate of the sorcerer's apprentice, everywhere things are spurting out, they jiggle, they Jacques. They dance. He is the dancer and condenser. Dancer with an *a* or with an *e* like denser. Circumdanscer. Not a word of his but yields to the least pressure of the jousting tongue and opens to the most unforeseen depths.

One last remark: this work of his is tragic. It is on the verge of tears. It is haunted by mourning, regret, inconsolation. Yet it makes us burst out laughing. It's that it never stops playing tricks on us, catching us off guard, sending us up. Off we sail. It takes us in. We are led astray. Disconcerted.

He makes me laugh. Write laughing. And that laughing is another philosophical way of learning to die, this too he whispers to us in tears.

*That's Jewish you think?*

Right away, the first time on the mountain, I realized I had to take him at his word, to the letter, to the summit, literally, to the comma as well, without which the sparks wouldn't fly nor the water gush from his text, meticulously, being attentive to the point of finickiness. To the point as well.

I shall restrict myself or take to myself only a few words or letters here, taking him then by words with words, trusting as he himself so often has to the luck of the draw, if there is such a thing.

"At random" then I draw one of the books standing in front of me. It is *Circumfession*.

❖ ❖ ❖ ❖ ❖ ❖ ❖ ❖ ❖ ❖

It all begins on the stroke of a Name with his Name for which he is not answerable he declares my name my very own but of which I am not the author, not even the keeper, at best the kept, his given name, to which he answers, but for which he does not answer. Whatever this name might do—in his life or his unconscious or out in the world—whatever this name might do in his name, it is not his fault, too bad if he does not answer for it, it's his lot his whole name, and nothing he can do about that. He doesn't even name it when he mentions it (in period 10 for a start), so as to assert his constitutive irresponsibility, his, and by the same token that of his name, the name that passes for him, speaks for him, signs in his place, in place he insists of the *replacement* or substitute that he is, as a son, one son in the series of sons, all mortal naturally, but he alone alive as replacement, him living with two dead at his side one ahead and one behind, him keeping the place of the lost sons for his mother, living for three, one living and two dead, he never thinks of it without trembling and shrinking from the impossible replacement, but tormented in his imagination, implacable poet of the unconscious, imagining his mother loves him instead of another, he is not the one she so tremulously loves he is the one she believes she loves in trembling for another. He believes. The first tragedy, it is this innocent mistaking of love it is this primal scene acted by faceless characters, a scene in which love and mourning are all mixed up, where the hero is all the more cherished as he is the body of another as well. That dying and love are indissociable common root and cause, his family destiny has so disposed.

The story must first and foremost and before him have been *a story of sons*, not of brothers. His brothers—and he is said to have had a number of them, how many?—are not brothers. They are his mother's sons. Later the story will continue *in (his) sons*, sons of the tremulous father that he came to be forever the same, fearful, child, afraid of tears, afraid of crying, of causing tears, of being wept over and of not being wept. Afraid of act 2's judgment, love, circumcision, and uncircumcision. But in act 1 the tears fears and weeping belong to the mother.

It is his lot to be one in a series, the one kept to the right of death and kept from death on the left as well.

❖  ❖  ❖  ❖  ❖  ❖  ❖  ❖  ❖  ❖  ❖

For whom did the mother weep, does she weep and will she weep, *literally* [*à la lettre*]? *Literally* is what concerns our poet, a caller of language and the unconscious to account, hyperpunctilious, a hyperformalizer, a surreptitious mathematician of moods. Here's how he torments himself to the letter (to the comma as well): the son in him—hence one-of-the-sons, one-off-the-sons [*un défils*] and therefore doomed to a deficit of love—fearstrembles no doubt and this fearer regrets not having the slightest chance of being mourned, he Jackie, mourned *to the letter*, to the j, a, c, k, i, e—but into this same sigh slips, I am not an egotist, I do not want what I want, I want to spare my mother an excess of suffering, already she has mourned two sons that's enough, twice for all, he claims, he lies, he makes believe. And yet there is more truth in this allegation than in all of philosophy. In truth, unthinkable, at each death we mourn the same person or the same death, we relive the loss of the first of our loved ones. "It is always the child we lose," I said once (in *Déluge*), whether the one to depart be father, mother, daughter, or son, at each death it is *the child* itself we lose in tears, the child each person dying becomes, the child that, departing, you who are going away, awake in me whom you abandon all in tears. Before the mother's bereft visage there is always nothing but a son. He, Jacques Derrida in his wisdom and divination, knowing this, she, his mother never having known it an innocent illiterate and not the sort to put a name or her finger on the place where it hurts. And since she does not know and does not say, it is he who, here as elsewhere,

thinks it out in place of the mother, an intruder into the maternal unconscious, implicated not from indiscretion but from chagrin, a son in the skein
of sons. There he is in the snarl, there he is tangled up with others, sons
fathers, he himself loses the thread, the sons, just as she does: it would be an
excess of suffering to weep over *him*, *him* in place of me, I who am sometimes
the first sometimes the third person in this teary-eyed scene, him-me, who
comes along after the dead one, who comes therefore from the dead, comes in
place of the dead, me received begot conceived as supernumerary and
revenant and all dripping with death. One more son, she must think he
thinks, a son to lose, he thinks she must be thinking, although what can he
know about that? But he thinks it all the same. Born condemned. "One mortal too many," is his idea. Of hers. Him the occupant, the replacement, *hence
the replaced*. "I saw then the first mourning as the mourning of my mother who
could not therefore literally weep for me, me the sole replacement," he reit-
erates what he wants-believes to be. As if there were such a thing as *the sole
replacement*! Everyone replaced except for him? Or perhaps: there is only one
replacement, one substitute running around replacing all the dead? Or
maybe: I alone do not have a place I alone can reside only at the *re*-place. As
for the place, I'm not taking it, I'm giving it back. All mourned. Except for
him. When suddenly the phone rings. He flies to his mother's bed. Nice, tie,
suit "trying in vain not only to weep but ( . . . ) to refrain from weeping, *et
fletum frenabam* (and I restrained my tears)." "In vain" being common to weeping and not weeping, one can't decide whether he did or didn't weep. This is
the origin of the undecidable . . .

"trying ( . . . ) to elude all programs and quotations," is an explanation of
what he is trying to do, he tries at the same time to weep and to refrain from
weeping, he wants to avoid whatever is the expected thing in a given situation. Is the code: I must weep, or is the code, as for Saint Augustine, his other
brother and most cherished predecessor, I must refrain from weeping? He is
always one step ahead, if people are weeping, I will not weep, if people refrain

from weeping, I must not refrain from weeping. Is it possible to remain out-side all programs? I would say: no but yes. As he shows, by writing with such mobility, with such shifts in meaning, with such quick syntactical changes that one cannot say to him: aha, you are weeping; as a matter of fact, no, I am not weeping, ah, you refrain from weeping; not at all I do not refrain from weeping. And his sentence describes the movement that animates the unde-cidable. The undecidable is not a clean break is a quick leap between two opposing possibilities but that touch. His internal movement is always to be where you least expect him. As if in response to his mother who in the end was expecting him without expecting him. This child has come along, another has just died, he comes from this having just come to go away again, always he turns up where you least expect him. One goes looking for him, he eludes all the programs of tears and quotations. And calmly announces: "when the unforeseeable did not fail to occur." He doesn't say, when the unforeseeable occurs, the door opens, and Derrida strides in. No, he says the unforeseeable never fails, that what fails never fails, you can count on blindly.

Why does he want to elude quotations, and not only programs, conven-tions, laws, interpretations, readings? He wants *to elude quotations* because he is himself originally a quotation. *He is a quotation of his brothers*, his mother's sons, trying to escape the destiny that goes with his birth like circumcision, giving quotation the slip through the doorway of syntax. How to get out of the family programming one son then a son then another son, which means his mother can no longer weep for him, because if she had to weep for him, it's not sure that she would be weeping for him, it might be for the one before or the one after, the tears in any case are wasted, he will not be mourned. The tearful letters follow him around and there is no stanching them. The solu-tion is hidden in the language in the sleights of hand of his writing. How to escape when the unforeseeable didn't fail to happen "surprising me absolute-ly but like what goes without saying, inflexible destiny, that is, incapable of recognizing me that evening." Who is incapable of recognizing whom? It must be *her*, the mother, thinks the reading, and we expect to see her take the place of the subject in the sentence when—surprise, improbable anacoluthon—it's not her but him, I, Jackie, the famous "sole replacement," who, without the least embarrassment, at break of day, takes her place—in the sentence, in the room thus: "incapable of recognizing me that evening and according to the doctors, having, only a few hours to live, at break of day ( . . . ) I arrived first in the white room." This indeed was unexpected! Who is (incapable) (resuscitated) in the place of whom in this story? We shall never know.

It remains to deplore what cannot be deplored, and to regret to no avail that in one way or another we are always replacements and substitutes. The first tragedy—by way of his surnames, given names and no-names, by what there is in a name, a story the whole story, every story. And so everything began, had begun with the given names, given as so often like blows, you are given it and nothing to be done, there you are named marked once and for all, put in the power of such and such a name, and sometimes there's a name, and that name is clearly exercising its occult powers and you haven't even been given it, you don't even know it has you, there it is working on (in) your shadow, behind your back, but it doesn't forget you *Elie, Elie* far-reaching in its consequences, here's the story resurfacing decades later as it emerges now, in the room of *Circumfession* where our hero turns around his mother's dying bed in this place and in this sacred (counter) time, which awaits us all if it hasn't found us already, where everything that has been left unsaid rises to the surface, too late and nonetheless *good* and late. It seems to take place in 1988 and simultaneously in 1976, in 1929, in 1930 in Africa and in France, this revelation, and entirely in the extraordinary French whose particularities here command great swaths of thought, for one thing the necessity of taking sexual differences of all sorts into consideration.

It's that the work of Jacques Derrida commences with a name given to a boy *with a feminine ending*. In the first place he was called *Jackie*. Later he called himself *Jacques*. In second place, and no doubt at the same moment, comes the other name, the Jewish name, the no-name, he says, the one that will remain hidden, a name both brief and immense, and it too this name this exclusively boy's name, this Eli*e* in French has a feminine ending, like Jacki*e*.

Here is what the author, the mother's earpiece in *Circumfession,* tells us about it on the phone in periods 16 and 10. The person who speaks here and says *I,* being a mixture of Jacques and of Jackie, of masculine and feminine, of son with mother.

> . . . and thus, a little while ago she pronounced my name [that is his ear-liest name, the "true" one, not that of the author], Jackie, echoing the sentence of my sister passing her the receiver, "hello Jackie," something she had not been able to do for months and will perhaps do no more, beyond the fact that throughout her life she scarcely knew the other name: "*Elie: my name—not inscribed, the only one, very abstract, that ever happened to me, that I learned, from outside, later, and that I have never* felt, borne, *the name I do not know, like a number (but what a number! a matricule . . . )."*

Matriculated, behind his back, LI in Roman numerals, 51 in Arabic numerals, but in which register exactly (matriculated being derived metaphorically from *mater*) was he inscribed unknown to everyone, it's one of those stories of belat-ed revelation-election, of revelection, one was enrolled without one's knowl-edge. Suddenly, tardily, the chosen, the elect without knowing it finds himself taken up or off, a sub*li*me and ever-dreadful kidnapping. Benediction strikes. So he had gone his way bearer of the order that destined him to the secret, to the separation, obedient to the unread letter, as always, and the order was: you shall bring down the idol of authority you shall deconstruct, you are come to disorganize order itself, you shall extract the ore, you shall make orphans of certitudes. You shall read [*liras*] languages right to the bone and you shall unread [*délireras*] them to the point of de*li*rium. In the name of the mother the son and Saint Augustine "and in this sense, more than any other, it is the given name, which I received without receiving it in the place where what is received must not be received, nor give any sign of recognition in exchange (the name, the gift), but as soon as I learned, very late, that it was my name, I put into it, very distractedly, on one side, in reserve, a certain nobility, a sign of election, I am he who is elected [*celui qu'on élit*], this joined to the story of the white tallith (to be told elsewhere) and some other signs of secret benediction" (23–12–76), my *escarre* [bedsore] itself.

Here too I read attentively watching for what happens to the skin and flesh of the text, incision, graft of a fragment lifted from another segment of time, one stitches it up again, the closed lips of the wound saying: *the other name . . . my escarre itself.* Scar, mortification, bedsore, this other name "not written down" but scored with a knife in the soul, memory-itself along with what is *eli*ded in forgetting.

It turns up again, Elie, the *escarre*, immediately afterward, in period 17, this time linked to the 1976 notebooks, to the very gesture of writing, Elie writes,

my secret name, Elie, around which the first notebooks from 1976 circled, drawing pads with thick leaves whose cover bore an *escarre*, that is, a coat of arms with two lions, an open square around whose edges one could read the words *skizze, croquis, sketch, schizzo, schets, kpoki*, and I added by hand, in Hebrew, the word for word, מילה, pronounce it *milah*, which names the word and circumcision, trying to find out already whom at bottom Elie would have loved, from whom, "last loved face," he would have chosen to receive his name like an absolution at the end of a confession without truth . . .

*Elie* is there then, always has been, as soon as he begins to write, as a repeated scar, the wound, the word, the word for the wound. The name of the word to write in every tongue: *Ecrire, Scribere, Schreiben, Graben. To Write: to open the tomb, to bury*, to give oneself up to reading in secret.

And so he was Elie, one or other of the Elies, male, female, each and every one of the Elies, and unaware of it. But Elie knew he was Elie. The Elect. *Elie*, in French. Elie who like all prophets is elected so as not to be read. L, I—I, L—L, elle: "I should not wear any outward Jewish sign." Not outward. Only in secret.

❖ ❖ ❖ ❖ ❖ ❖ ❖ ❖ ❖ ❖

Elie it is! meaning read and link, and elect and I and she, LI, the *Y* at the end of *La Double Séance* so he reads himself right to the lees Elie Elie Elie . . . [*Elie Eh! lis, et lie, élit, et lit, et l'I, elle y, LI, l'Y . . . hèle I il se lit . . . jusqu'à la lie*]. He reads this name of Elie, which links him to litera-ture, to elect, to lie, to bed, child-bed deathbed, and to all of the Elies, if one elides it makes *zélie* in French, zealous, this line of Elies, Elie author of delicts unmentioned or elided in the family, as one no longer mentions the name of Uncle Eugene Elie "since the day he abandoned wife and children to make himself a new life in the metropolis" but we don't talk about that for fear of attracting the "devil" at the tail end of period 35, we must forget about him. Elie, elided by his mother's withdrawal into silence: "when I ask her, how many times will I have asked her this: 'who am I?', it's as though for you I'd changed my name without her knowing and my presence then finally becomes the absence it always was."

Couldwould she have answered this question "whose syntax suddenly appears to me to be incredibly difficult to understand in a mirror, when the circulation of blood in the brain is impaired, 'who am I?', and I imagine her protesting in silence, impotent and impatient faced with the incorrigible nar-cissism of a son who seems to be interested only in his own identity, but no, that of his double, alas, the dead brother" (period 27).

Who am I, me, me in my place in the presence of myself somewhere I have never been, the impossible question, cut in two, I and me, insatiable dolor of the foundling, dolor of the double, double dolor. Elie his trespasser's name, the family misfit. A phantom lacking all the qualities of a phantom. A phantom infantom. What the devil, he'd say, derrridevilishly.

*I don't know how long we've had family names says my mother, Eve Klein, Klein, in the old days this must have corresponded to the size of the people or to their importance. No one knows where they come from. Not me anyway. Because they've been around for a long time, these names—it's the least of my worries. —Whose is it? I say. We don't know. Says my mother. There are so many things we don't know.*

# III

## OF THE KLEINS AND THE GROSSES

As Jacques Derrida recalled one day in a note in *Voiles*—another sub*li*me book with tal*li*th and trimmed in the imminence of death—yet another reverie of a so*li*tary Jewish traveler—as he recalled in *Voiles*, the name of my own maternal grandfather the German ex-Austro-Czechoslovakian who died for Germany was Michael Klein, my mother is a Klein, Klein as in Klein, Klein the name and *klein* the word, Klein, Klein the Klein of *Gespräch im Gebirg*, the first cousin-on-the-female-side of Gross, Klein as the German Jews were called, or else Gross, it's all the same, called in German with German words what could be more ordinary and more German, called Little or Big, whether or not one is big, little, for the Jew nothing is proper, everything is lent and borrowed, the Jew's proper name has nothing proper about it in which I quote Celan, and his wink of a smile, saying that the Jew came along, and with him came his name, his unpronounceable name, *"und mit ihm ging sein Name, der unaussprechliche . . . "* With, separately.

As my grandmother used to say, *die kleine Frau Klein*, little Mrs. Klein (Little), who always went off before me, *mit meinen Beinem* (with my legs), accompanied by her legs, and did not just go as I myself went. From her I learned the motif of the autonomy of the parts of the whole, starting with the name.

—What do you mean? we say, what makes Klein or Big or Little unpronounceable or Elie even, but says Celan, it is, however pronounceable it may be, Elie he is, the unnameable, the Jew, look what he gets, the Jew, a name, and hardly has he got it but it becomes effectively unpronounceable for non-Jews, as unpronounceable as a name like Cixous or Derrida. So what does the child, the poet, the Jew, to whom one says: you there, what's this name, this foreign name, this repulsive name, do? He takes it, he takes up the name and he does not rest until he has de-nominated it, broken it down patched it up turned it around, sowed yes left it in the dust and cut and crossed it until all the seed has been squeezed out, the sperm, the letters of a work. If Jacques Derrida has disclosed the fabulous workings of Genet pricking out his name and all its letters with such extreme sensitivity it is that he was predisposed by his own elective grafts.

For what can Jewish children "like the two cousins in Celan's *Jud und Sohn eines Juden,* claim as their own, not a thing really, *das nicht geborgt wär, ausgeliehen und nicht zurückgegeben ist* even their shadow is foreign," says Celan, even their given name, assigned, that is, lent, flayable, detachable and yet and with good reason so cherished, yes so flesh of their flesh even their name does not belong to them. Hence Jewish boys have two given names, the non-Jewish name, their official birth-certifiable name and the other one, the Jewish name, which sometimes, as was often the case in Algeria, they will never use and may not even know about.

Throughout her life she scarcely knew the other name: *"Elie: my name—not inscribed, the only one, very abstract, that ever happened to me, that I learned, from outside, later, and that I have never* felt, borne, *the name I do not know, like a number (but what a number! I was going to say* matricule, *thinking of the plaque of the dead Elie that Marguerite wears or of the suicide, in 1955, of my friend Elie Carrive) anonymously designating the hidden name, and in this sense, more than any other, it is the* given *name, which I received without receiv-*

*ing in the place where what is received must not be received, nor give any sign of*
*recognition in exchange (the name, the gift), but as soon as I learned, very late,*
*that it was my name, I put into it, very distractedly, on one side, in reserve, a*
*certain nobility, a sign of election, I am he who is elected* [celui qu'on élit]."

(PERIOD 16)

And that's why Jacques Derrida claims to be dissociated from this initial
hallmarking, the starting point from which there is no setting off, of which
he has been robbed, which nettles him.

Chance or arbitrariness of the starting point, irresponsibility even, you
will say, inability I still have to answer for my name, even to give it back
to my mother . . .

(PERIOD 10)

The name received without being received, given without his knowledge,
like the symbol of the wound also administered to the body in spite of itself—
the *milah* the circumcision—the other name his name of other, my scar itself,
the badge that sets me apart (but what does it mean to be a scar?). My badge,
which loves me, *un escarre beau* as the nurse said you recall, she was certain that
such a deep and mordant wound must be masculine in gender. My cockchafer,
such a lovely avatar, my scarab. All the coleoptera of Egypt enter with Elie
here. Let us join them in their peregrinations, being forever interrupted, covered up, put in parentheses, in quarantine, in brackets, throughout period 17,
which mimics this chronicle of successive relegations.

*"The fact that this forename was not inscribed {on my birth certificate, as were the*
*Hebrew names of my family} (as though they wanted to hide it, still more than*
*the other Hebrew names, placed after the others), was as though effaced, held back,*
*signified several things mixed together: first of all that they wanted to hide me like*

*a prince whose parentage is provisionally concealed to keep him alive (I've just thought, trying to explain this gesture to myself [my parents never talked to me about it, I never asked them about it, it remains secondary and occupies so much space here only because of the thread I have chosen to follow] that a brother died when a few months old, less than a year before my birth, between my elder brother, René [Abraham], and me. He was called Paul Moses), keep him alive until the day that his royalty could . . . be openly exercised, without risk for the precious semen; and then that I should not openly wear any Jewish sign"* (23–12–76).

Everything seems to have taken place as if, without his knowledge, the family had enacted a modern version of an ancient drama whose main character was one Moses or Oedipus of El-Biar or other.

In which one sees how the Goddess Substitution, or perhaps Superstition, is forever at her replacing, juggling with metonymy, and this one by that one Paul Moses by Elie loved in place of another, a good thing a bad thing, Elie in place of Moses, which of them to weep for, who does(will) she weep for when the time comes, weeping for Elie is it not Moses for whom she is (may be) weeping and she, who else is she, she who, already departed, comes back to her place, her proper place, standing in for herself for she is the figure of absolute survival, *inc* [*s.a.*]., the corporation of absolute survivors, survivors anonymous, herself *s. a.* as on the same page Saint Augustine, S. A., son, holy man, him and her, each of them experiencing in turn the infinite replacement, bad-good-thing, *s.a.*, *without end* . . .

This being so, he is right to ask *how should I answer for my name*, you need to know which is whose, and who can hold himself and be held fully responsible, the game is up from the very first, game up game over, I—neither wholly Jacques Derrida nor Paul Moses either, a little Elie a little him [*il*] a little her [*elle*]—have nowhere to settle [*demeurer*] save in a state of incapacity. But for that two must die [*deux meurent*] one in the place of the other.

*Name, nom* from the French possessive *mon* read backwards. Dispossessive.

## Destinerrancy of the prophet Jackie Baba d'El-Biar . . .

Elijah, the name of the one who gets carried away, elevated over the head of his pupil Elisha who also aspired to Elysium, Elie (2 Kings), Elie the name he has never borne, his phantom name but in French—for if it came late, Elie, he who receives it—one no longer knows who receives whom in the ancient circus of hospitality—makes the most of its letters and imaginative effects in French. Elie, what an astounding character, the first by that name, the magical, the one in whose ear *the word* whispers—god telephones him inwardly, you remember the story, at first he cannot hear the voice of God, which doesn't mean he doesn't hear God he hears God-the-noise, God-the-ruckus, and finally, *in the end* he hears—he hears absolutely—he hears—. Period. The voice of God who does not speak, who speaks God. Period, end of sentence. Elie the one who can talk to God in the noise, in the silence, in the word that says nothing—nothing human. Only the dead can bear the grandeur of this terribly small voice. Elie who fleeing death, went a day's journey into the wilderness, went and adjourned himself under a juniper tree and says I am dead I want to die I've had enough God enough. Then he falls asleep and an angel comes who says to him eat. Elie's the one who says I am dead and rises like a cake. Like someone who believing he's been new-made grows himself a new skin. The one fed on command by ravens, then by the widow, the nourisher, the parter of rivers rainmaker, bringer of rain to the face of the earth, this toppler of kings is also, this is what particularly strikes him, him Elie-Jacques-Derrida, *the hospitaller*, present at each circumcision. You see the picture: Elie present at the circumcision of Elie otherwise known as Jackie held on Elie's lap. This scene has a double hallucinated in Derrida's phantasmagorical museum: the burial of Count Orgaz (period 29). Elie, the one my grandmother Granny Reine Cixous of Oran was expecting every Friday evening, the table laid in the house of the widow, haunted him before any knowledge of it. He was there at the door, years before Jacques Derrida heard about it. See where he turns up in *Schibboleth*, this Elie, but with the name of Elie concealed in the word Sh*i*bbo*l*eth, and the prophet in the poet Celan, but never, at any moment, does Jacques Derrida the commentator breathe a word of his own connivance with Elie the first in these elliptical pages.

And so he paints a secret self-portrait setting the other up in in his place of the other, but the resemblance is flagrant:

> A word open to whomever may also be concerned in the figure, perhaps, of some prophet Elie, of his phantom or double. He is hard to recognize, through this monstration of the monster, but one must know how to recognize him. Elie is the one to whom hospitality is due, promised, prescribed. He can come, one must be aware, at any moment. He can make an event of his coming at any moment.
>
>      . . .
>
> The prophet Elie, Celan does not name him, it didn't occur to him perhaps. I also risk recalling that Elie is not only the guest, the one to whom the door of a word must open, as the *relationship* itself. Elie is not only a messianic or eschatological prophet. God has commanded, tradition says, that he be present at each circumcision, each time, every time. He watches over them.
>
>                                              (*Schibboleth*, PP. 102–103)

So I, Klein, ask Gross him—always this desire to talk and ask questions, the pair of them—Celan says—

—You've come a long way up here, with your name.

—I have come.

—And so when did this name of Jacques come to you?

—When I published *The Origin of Geometry* says Gross the Big. It was *evident* that I couldn't publish under the name of Jackie, you understand?

—I understand say I, Klein as I am. The evidence of the avoidance.

—My American identity is Jacques. Jackie is used in the family, says Gross.

—I understand, *versteh ich*, say I in my other language. *Bist ja gekommen von weit, bin ja gekommen wie du.*

They go at it for a good long while. I must let them jabber. But before I'd like to hang around in the vicinity of this meeting on the *Gebirg* for a bit, long enough to underscore the poetic indication left by Celan, I quote in German this sentence Jacques Derrida quotes in French in *Voiles*, p. 36.

*kam, kam, gross, kam dem andern entgegen, Gross kam auf Klein zu, und Klein, der Jude, heiss seinen Stock schweigen vor dem Stock des Juden Gross.*

And I note the strangeness of the chiasmus: Klein, the Jew, and the Jew Gross. The figure of the meeting that takes effect in the sentence: thus Celan, like Jacques Derrida everywhere, plays here on difference and on identity. It is in working with the variations, in the rhythm and syntax of the language, that they point up the differences between things that are alike and even the same. What difference is there between Klein the Jew and the Jew Gross, each of whom comes along with his mark of a Jew, comes before and after comes? I take the lesson to heart: if Jew there is it is always with a difference, always different, and always in the *différance* and in the Jewerrance. *N.B.* I take this lesson to heart: that which is always with difference does not equal Jewish. Differences in the differences.

I take up my stick again and it speaks of Jackie and of Jacques, Jacques with *que* and with *s*, Jacques with the silent sign of the plural in French and Jackie with his *i* and his mute *e*, his feminine *silenced* and his American *ck*, Jackie a period name, the period when Algeria's Jewish families, naive, native, were infatuated with foreign names especially the Anglo-American ones. They just loved Jack, William, Pete, and the vocables conjured up by fantasies of a promised land other than France, longed for but increasingly explicitly hostile. I am speaking of the years 1930 to 1950 in Algeria. All that magic shibbolethery so as to try and get across the border into Eldorado, United States, imaginary clandestine passengers drifting their dreams down Bab Azoun Street or in the Lyre marketplace. So he was elected Jackie, as my grandfather named his Oran hat shop *Highlife* pronounced "Iglif," Jackie like Jackie Koogan the Kid, Jackiderrida, that's him all right, take a gander not everyone sees him. Jackid in his outsize cap, always ready to pick a fight. Jackie like *j'acquis* get it? and *jacqui* get who? with *a* and *i* he notes in period 8.

❖  ❖  ❖  ❖  ❖  ❖  ❖  ❖  ❖  ❖

*A, i* [ pronounced *haï*, as in "hated"] he says, in such a loud voice, and all of a sudden he catches himself, hating whom he had loved, oto-analyst, oto with two *o*'s spoken aloud.

*A, i*, and always the inaudible *e*.

*A, i* and *e* also as in Jackie and Janine (of the name not named) and *e, i, a* as in Derrida and in Marguerite. Always that French feminine *e* at the end, smuggled in, opening him to others, and time and again to this woman's voice vying with him for death [*la mort*], taking the bit [*le mors*] in French—right up to the agony of her death in Nice, *a, i, ai, aïe*—

And God! I was going to forget about him. Besides, he too remembers God (period 23). Well, well! It is not a name that often crosses his lips, the lord of the Shechinah presence, in whom he confesses not believing, he admits to God that believing is not his strong point, not his weakness either, but for a name there is always a place, in him, in his name the name of Jacques Derrida. God the name dwells in his name, behind the curtain, in French. A name that finds grace in his eyes because of its first syllable in French, *Di eu dit du d'yeux, Dieu,* a good player this word god. It's another of his mother's words (period 23). As for God, Saint Augustine's, the absolute witness, God the One who is not born and to whom, as he observes in *Foi et Savoir*, we speak in Latin, even in French, God who Latins our tongues, the God of the religion that is the response he reminds us, the absent one in his place, in other words the empty place, here in a few words is how he describes the Great Hypothetical:

> God: the witness as "nameable-unnameable," the present-absent witness of all possible oaths or pledges. Supposing, *concesso non dato*, religion had any connection whatsoever with what we name thus God, it would belong . . . to a history of the *sacramentum* and of the *testimonium*. It would be this history, it would be mixed in with it. On the boat . . .
>
> (*Foi et Savoir*, p. 40)

God if he is is thus God, obviously: insidious. But the God of whom he likes to think, is the one who retracts, the *Unheimlich*, the unpredictable, the giving thundering God of the Bible—the one who talks with Elie, Noah, and the rest of them.

I have spoken of his Names [*Noms*]. The time has come to speak of his No's [*Nons*], as dictated by the homonymy that enlivens the French language, as suggested also, through curious connivances, by Jacques Derrida's profound and instinctive rejection of all attempts to take power through the drive to appropriate, no sooner dislodged than it is reestablished. And of the Theme of Sovereignty. Well, no, he says, no he affirms, to be more precise, there is always one of him who tries to say and to affirm, by dipping—each time that he is pressed to accept or, to borrow that magic word, to *consent* that is to feel *cum*, with, to enter into *cum*, into community, into *comme*-unity—into "his stock of no's."

"Consent," another of those devious words in French, rich in the effluvium of reticence. What a deal of ruse, unconscious or not, what a deal of unavowed resignation. One never consents, especially him, except as they say of a ship's mast, or of the yard that is forced to yield and bend. So many no's in his yes's. True, his circonsentments are not a matter of temperament but of philosophical attitude, foreseeing and fearing as he always does each time he accepts an invitation, the almost inevitable crystallization with its alluring appearance of community drifting too quickly into the illusion of shared identity—hence the dose of surrender that insinuates itself into the consent, the *cum*, cumpromise, the compromise, the as-promised. As if he perceived in each aggregation of people the menace of some theatrical travesty. A sort of cavern where he would be kept seated in the role of Socratic guest.

He would like to say *no* without its being violent, *no*, out of respect for each other you not like me. In any case he says it philosophically, this no of distinction, this warning, ceaselessly refining the propositions and terms of the problem, with delicate gestures, saying it's not so simple, making use of the notsosimplicity, it is not exactly that, to himself as to his interlocutors, a no that doesn't reject, that doesn't deny but that opens, a humble wicket, onto the *space* between foreign shores where the human elements that we are or believe ourselves to be move about, sometimes mingling, mixing together, sometimes differentiated. No, I am not you he murmurs, I am not me either, however it sometimes happens that I be you or you traverse me. Here it remains to recall the name forever withdrawn from oblivion by Jacques Derrida of this *Ni* that does not deny. *Ni*, the name of Nothing, which does not annihilate. It remains to recall on the verge of the time of times this chora without qualities, without properties,

the place name, *a* place name, and a very singular one, for *this* spacing that, not letting itself be dominated by any theological, ontological or anthropological instance, ageless, history-less and more "ancient" than all oppositions (for example sensible/intelligible), does not even proclaim itself as "beyond being," according to a via negativa. Consequently, *chora* remains absolutely impassive and heterogeneous to all processes of historical revelation or anthropotheological experience that suppose nonetheless its abstraction. It will never have entered into religion and will never allow itself to be made sacred, sanctified, humanized, theologized, cultivated, historialized. Radically heterogeneous to the safe and sound, to the saint and the sacred, it does not allow itself to be *indemnified*. . . . It will always resist them, it will always have been (and no future anterior, even, will have been able to reappropriate, change the direction of or reflect a *chora* with neither faith nor law) the *place* itself of infinite resistance, of an infinitely impassive remainingness: an utterly other and without face.

(*Foi et Savoir*, P. 31)

Had it not had a name? But it does have one, a Greek name, which contrary to the name of God is not translated into any language, otherwise he would have invented it, he needs *chora,* this Chora, this abstract verbal character that *seems* to us by phonic play to have a body [*corps*] in French, this icon of language, whose omnipotence without the least power only makes her all the more absolutely powerful. Next to her, God *is*. While she is the completely other. Aura of the faceless.

He lives his entire philosophy, his life, in their indescribable interval; one cannot see them face to face, but one can, in dreams, encounter them.

## IV

## THE DREAM OF NAÏVETÉ

Let us stay with his mother a while, for we shall be hard put to exhaust our discoveries concerning the extent of her involvement, although she never intended to be involved, with the whole of the work, with the destiny, with the son, with the spirit, and in a poignant and inaugural fashion, with the writing itself. *Circumfession* makes us aware of this in its incredible manner, fluid, nearly ungraspable but legible to the fairly naked eye, she is in on it from the start, naive, wily, full of a redoubtable innocence she's the image of her son, she whom he sometimes calls G., sometimes my mother, sometimes Georgette spelled out, and whom her brother called Geo, Jo—as in Jo-seph you might think it a man's name, Geo written Geo—like Geof, like Geography like Gaia, our ancestor the Earth, it's her in every genre and gen-der, the more one reads her, the more one revolves around her bed with him the more our eyes and ears discover the tremendous import of the tie between this mother and this son, between this earth and this universe, between she who opens all the veins of the text, as we shall read in *Circumfession*, from the very first period, and he who with her and without her with/out her, with his blood of hers and of his, in this sublime book and beyond conceives a hither-to unheard of version of a double primal scene.

I said "his mother" but who is the mother, who is his mother, and who is, what is this mother, because of whom he has written, he could not not have written this loveliest of prayer books, the book errant, the grief-stricken book turned around the survival bed, what is a mother and how does one recognize the being called mother how does he recognize her as his mother, how does he recognize her for a mother? In that she does not recognize him, in that she has always notrecognized him, that is, recognized without annexing him, in that she has always held him in this floating vague unrecognition, in that she does not hear him, in that she does not flee from him, does not grasp him does not read him lets herself be called, called, lets him call her to call him, call on her to call on him, G. absolutely does not quote him, raise the stakes [*relancer*], does not return the question that troubles him right to the end, by what she accomplishes in his or her place, the mystery of the absent presence, the unostentatious celebration of the daily agony, hers, the tenuous tenacious incarnation of the art of losing, she is the one who makes him speak, while he believes it is he who is trying to make her speak, this "impassibility of a time beyond time" whom he resembles increasingly he says they say whom he fears resembling, not resembling, increasingly, fearing increasingly, the mute god the beast, increasingly hard-pressed, pressing, with a presentiment of the resemblance in store.

Enter she whom he confesses confessing himself, in precarious confessions, all the more moving as they are nearly mute, only a few words but what words! and they are going to fall silent.

Brief ameoba songs, telegraphy in utmost proximity, the canon, trembling with anguish, of the great separants, uttered with the air of one who is searching for something someone who is there, here, a name, *where was I who am I me I ache for my mother because I am charming I'm losing what does that mean I don't know Jackie what are you thinking about*—à *qui?* of whom? *nobody* signed nobody—of whom—and silence is the rest, silence, she remains. *A qui* . . . ackie. *Je tu* . . . hush . . . hush.

And on the one hand the writer who fears dying before the end of a long sentence, on the other the son who fears seeing her die before the end of the confession—his mother, the sentence—before she has confessed (it), before he has confessed her, before she has before he has, avowed—but what? Always the crime, the cause, the origin, the filiation, the inheritance, trembling also to depart before his mother, she whom he does not write on, he does not write on Geo, nor on Saint Georgette, nor on Esther, her sacred name, she too has another name, a non-name, and what a name, a sacred name, Esther, she is queen without knowing it and for Jews, what a queen, the noble, the beautiful, the kind, the savioress, bestower of survival, and all unbeknownst to her. Everything going for her and for the Jewish people. And what's more, espoused to a non-Jew . . . in any case, in the Book.

Esther, whom he loves. And for what? He had already confided this (to us) in *La Carte Postale*. On the fateful date of 7 September 1977, playing the sevens, his and the one Esther conceals in her name, in her signature, playing on all possible *sevens* [*sept cet cette set sceptres*] that is on all the combinations of the number of her name, caballing for fun and for good, he agrees to unveil a corner of the secret: what ties him to her, the queen, the second one, a replacement, it's all to do with letters. All Jewish children are brought up on the milk of this fabulous tale, which, as he recalls, manages just fine without God. Here's the story, its specter, its remains: Esther, under the guidance of her uncle Mordecai, saves her people (from whom she is separated by marriage after which she is tied to them like never before, in secret, as if by yet another seven, that of incest)—from the death sentence that Haman, the vizier, minister custodian of the will and seal of the king, has wheedled out of his master. Thus begins a race against the letter, of letters, between letters, letter against letter, a gallop, a hunt, a roundup, a pursuit, a tracking down, a breathless staging on the theme of the Contretemps. The queen, forewarned and advised by her uncle M has such power of life that she does the impossible: suspends death, intercepts the order, returns the letter the fate to its sender, turns back time. Whereupon enter Jacques Derrida for whom this book of Esther was written for all time, he takes delivery of the missive and he reads, as follows, in all haste, it's his destiny:

> Then Mordecai tells Esther: about the sum of money given to Haman, about the decree a "copy" of which he has had sent to her. What Esther manages to do then, is stop death—"the decree of death" . . . Esther stops the massacre by rerouting a letter, is what it amounts to. She stops, she intercepts (though it was necessary she *be there*, it was necessary Esther find herself in the letter's passage). She puts another in its place— for the countermand, the one that "is written to reverse the acts of Haman's scheme . . . this reversal occasions the identical writing scene: the royal seal, the decrees, the "posts on horseback" "being hastened and pressed on by the king's commandment," . . . what . . . interests me most at present: it is what links these death decrees, these letters that give and suspend death, what links them to *luck*, good and bad, to the writing of chance, of destiny, of fate, of prediction insofar as it casts a spell, casts lots. . . . For the feast of Esther (*Purim*) is a feast of lots. Haman . . . "had cast *Pur*—that is the lot—to destroy them and to cause them to perish." "Wherefore they called these days Purim/ . . . "
>
> It is written according to all that Haman had commanded/ to the king's governors, and the rulers of every people of every province,/ . . . according to the writing thereof,/ . . . written in the name of king Ahasuerus, and sealed with the king's ring./ The decrees are sent by posts/ . . . to exterminate, to kill and to cause to perish/ all Jews, both young and old, little children and women, in one day. . . . A copy of the writ to be given as a commandment in every city.
>
> (*La Carte Postale*, P. 80)

Of this story with its feminist overtones and racist rebounds Jacques Derrida keeps the letters of names and of words, he tosses the blood, the massacres of innocents to the winds he retains the fantastic vocable *Pur*, or *Pour* in French, a word that he allows to flow from meaning to meaning in French and for which like the great poet he is he provides a well-merited fate in all his texts. *Pour(for)*: in favor of, *pour*: instead of and therefore in dis-favor of: *pour*: in exchange; *pour*: in the direction of, destined to, *pour* with a view to, by reason of, as a consequence, all these *pours* for his great good fortune, which he can only however delight in in French, providing [*pourvu*] one is willing to listen to him.

Esther, written without an *h* (in French) as he points out, Ester *e, s, t, e, r*, the letters of a name I have used so much, so it will *rest* in us, says he, for he says it all, or at least it is all said by [*par*] him, and by him revealed, which does not ever mean that what is revealed *by* him, by the letters he uses, *dont il se sert, s, e, r, t,* is revealed *to* him, it is even almost the contrary, everything has always been written by him, through him starting with the name of Elie but he is perhaps the last to have read it. This blindness is not peculiar to him, he who writes does not read, one does not write to oneself, one tells oneself everything one confesses to oneself and one does not hear: that's what writing is, to be one's own [*s'être*] blind seer.

Esther, *e, s, t, e, r*, in French, like *ester en justice*, to go to court, as a woman may do, stand in a court of law without her husband's authorization. Ester like the essence of a perfume's fragrance. But let us come back to Esther who does not write but bears his letters, I mean her son under a pseudonym, Ester rest, *r, e, s, t, e* Esther is him in reverse, *reste* is his word, that's what matters to him after all, the remains [*reste*], to remain and *rest* as in English. One word, a handful of letters five or seven and of them he makes mountains of books. He can do anything with *reste*.

Take *Glas*: towers of rests and remains is what he builds up and knocks down by transplanting the elements of names and the roots of the passions of other youth born [*jeunes nés*] of other queens than him, Genet for one. Again and again, he shows us that we think and create as well and to begin with letters, sounds, the *gl* the *j* the *s* the *c*, etcetera, and with *ra* also if need be with the help of the homosynonymical magic, one can never say it often enough to ensure that it be heard for once.

I said he doesn't write on her. But he writes beside her, with her letters, around her, from her inexhaustible wellspring, from El-Biar (well in Arab) the earth that she is cracked open by his waters by his constant unfurling. He writes, she falls silent, is this to silence [*est-ce taire*] the mother or to speak for her? For—*pour*—the pur of purim . . . For Esther who spoke for her people. *Pur*—the lot. Each of us, the lot of the other. Each of us emerges from the other.

And here we are, bent over the banks of the maternal river and we find this twig, this stone, this sprout, so everything was in Esther this mother so different from the mother of S. A. A saint but somewhat given to drink. A mother, his peerless mother, and the mother, yes, bearer or not and all unintentionally, of his philosophical ocean. *Ursache*. Original cause he is often a little wistful.

Here I note what he has confided to us by way of comic Judaism: ester, the letters of a name I have so often utilized in order that it may remain, comma—(keep your eye on the commas, those tiny rods, mistresses of his innumerable amphibologies and anacoluthons, hence of such ambiguities as poke holes in the subject, in the literal meaning of things)—*in order that it remain*, comma, play on the interpolated clause—*for my mother was not a saint*, comma, *not Catholic in any case*. Says he, for he likes to play innocent, the euphemist, the naïf and at the same time be the cat's-paw of French. In-any-case-not-Catholic [*pas catholique*; that is, unorthodox], he remains. Maybe Jewish not really nor absolutely. But in any case not-Catholic never Catholic and forever a little unorthodox. What could be more manifest? It's an unorthodox unCatholic case.

I am back with his mother. I am in the dying room, in Nice, where he dares to write what he fears to write and fears not to write, breath after breath the wager of the end, the ends, of the love and of the writing, that which no one has ever been able to do, except in love and in dread, and in constant fear of the insinuation of murder or crime. But we never know who kills whom, who is silenced by whom.

I am in the room, I follow them both, mother and son in turn.

And what do I see? First that it is she who opens the vein of the text, who'd have thought it, it's not the father who's at the origin of the literature here, it's the mother, I've always said it, always known it, but careful it's the mother-who-doesn't-know-how (to give), the mother who doesn't follow, she doesn't read, she doesn't quote, she doesn't even say his name any longer, she doesn't call him, she's the one, the mother who makes him write, the one who in not quoting him does not give him the right to quote. She who from the very first period, to begin with, sets him off, gives him the blood and the word. Who in not giving him the name suppresses it. Overrates it. She looks vaguely elsewhere, has that powerful look of the great silent ones, she resembles Abraham in flashes, he who can no longer say anything to his son, who has no desire to say anything. He is there, in this room of her agony, in which there is a bed and an armoire, the chair he's sitting on is not in the text, the armoire, yes. He is with without her. He is with her, she is not with him. It's the very figure of love, of the vexed soul of love, what he calls the contretemps, it's the mourning scene itself they are playing, the love scene, that is, as the experience of the grief in joy, the solitude in union.

She is in her bed. I mean his book. Equivocal everything is eliquivocal.

He is not in her armoire. Oh! that armoire! He was sure he was kept there, he believed—did he believe?—that she'd kept his most precious and delicate armament in it, his letters, twice a week for thirty years, 2 x 30 x 52, 3,120 letters. or rather cards, he at any rate had kept a mental trace of them, the number, the letters he had confided to her, they were to be his legacy, what else could his poor mother have left him as legacy if not those delegated letters, those *destinerrants* sent off in trust they'd come back again. Oh! the tearful armoire! See him go, ssht, not a sound though she is almost not present, he rifles it from top to bottom, his mother's armoire, and now the oracle, *I am losing* makes unexpected sense, the *legtters* did she lose them? the cards?

We have already lived through this sad, surreptitious scene: it was in 1728. The one about to die under the eyes of a son she doesn't in the least recognize as such is Madame de Vercellis. The one who writes her letters, and who expects to be recognized if not during his lifetime then at least posthumously is Jean-Jacques Rousseau. This story of a fateful inheritance is recounted in the second book of *Les Confessions*. In this room the events that lead the disinherited young man to his work of genius are being accomplished. We are particularly well informed about the crime, the theft of a scrap of *ruban rose et argent déjà vieux*: it's the only thing we stole from the whole vast household inventory of the defunct Madame de Vercellis. A noble, unfeeling woman over whom we, on our side of the bed, have shed a quantity of heartfelt tears without her or anyone else taking note of them. An outpouring with nothing in return. We are about to lose her. She bequeaths a year of wages to the least of her servants. But we, who write *for* her, *not being listed as part of the household*, had nothing. *I got nothing* says Jean-Jacques, who finds himself naked. So he steals a scrap of pink ribbon, barely sufficient to cover up this circumcision. A tiny little bit of rosy substissue. Rose-pink. Had it not been rose and faded would he have bothered to take it? No. I shall have more to say concerning this *question of rose* below. The founding crime is committed, against his will. Which in turn engendered the accusation that we laid the blame for crime after crime at the door of the gentle Marion, which engendered the loss of this pearl, which engendered her fall, hers and his too, which engendered the aborted attempt to confess in *Les Confessions* and then again idem in *Les Rêveries du promeneur solitaire,* which engendered the subsequent attempts at *Confessions,* those of Stendhal, of Proust, of our own Jacques Derrida, and all of them confessed inexhaustibly, confessed in vain, inexhaustible vein.

But in the beginning it was all the fault of the lack of maternal "solicitude." It was his mother he wanted this Rousseau lad, the natural one, the one who would have given him the legacy of her milk [*le legs de son lait*]. Bequeathed the milk. The mother he'd have liked to smother with kisses. No such luck. Madame de Vercellis is all dried up and not a drop of legacy, the boy is not mentioned in the will, he alone is forgotten. So he helps himself poor thing and indeed very modestly getting himself back at that dried up bit of rose-pink umbilical cord.

Let us return to the bedroom in Nice. She keeps company with him in this very discreet drama, in this losingness in which they both describe the same human circle that passes through birth and death (*childbed bridebed deathbed*, says another son—Joyce at the bedside of his dying mother, but he's Catholic, not unCatholic).

In this circle where he turns around Georgette Sultana Esther the twice queen who turns now in the opposite direction now in the same there is an amazing mildness, he spoonfeeds his nursling, the daughter he never thought he would have, so late.

I close the door on the sublime couple. The armoire has done its work. It didn't keep his letters. Lost legacy. A backhanded gift to the one who discovered the caprices of destinerrancy. It was bound to happen that it happens that it is to him it doesn't arrive, loser take all, and losing wins. By means of this unwonted occurrence he enters the legend of the great mourning texts, engendered by the lack or default of a mother, Augustine, Rousseau, Proust, Derrida, those who would have liked, wantedfeared, contrary to all expectations, to be wept over by their mother.

*Is that Jewish, do you think?*

There is a close connection between circumcision and Mummy, this character unique in her kinds, an independent-minded powerful impotent old woman. Circumcision cuts; and she, the mother, cuts again, like the champion at overbidding she is, he knew it *from the very first page* she, circumcision, his mother, revives it in him and *exacerbates* it, it's as plain as the nose on my face he tells himself:

> the quoted time of this notebook pulls the white thread of a period cutting across the three others, at least, 1. the theolog*ic* program of SA, 2. the absolute knowledge or geolog*ic* program of G., and 3. the presently present survival or life by prov*isi*on of Georgette Sultana Esther, or Mummy if you prefer . . . a *s*ynchrony running the risk of hiding what's essen*t*ial, that is that the restrained confes*s*ion will not have been my fault but hers, as though the daughter of *Z*ipporah had not only committed the crime of my *ci*rcum*cisi*on but one more still, later, the first playing the kickoff, the original sin against me, but to reproduce itself and hound me, call me into question, me, a whole life long, to make her avow, her, in me.
>
> (PERIOD 14)

She is therefore his *recircumcision*. For his circumcision he wasn't around. For his *re*circumcision she's the one who's not there, that's what cuts it again for him.

And the book flows from this scene re-begun 59 times, where, like the Freudian slip signed by my own son, "the same circle will be circumcised in a maternal triangle," in 59 periods. Between January 1989 and April 1990 *Circumfession* will have had 59 *periods*, hence in a period of fifteen months four times as many periods as the average woman, as if it, Circumfession, had wished to speed up its cycles, pressed as it was by mortal imminence.

There it is, his primal scene. The one that is to engender his whole philosophy and his entire tragedy. She is there, she who has always not been with him, she is still there as ever not totally present but as never before. She, who no longer speaks his name, is the one who gives him the first word, *relance*, the bidding word, of this text, and it is from the cruelty [*cru-el/le*] of this moment, in its glowing tenebrae, that Jacques Derrida's dream, the *dream of dreams* of the signatory of so many books, is poured in the ear, the ear/eye—I should say of the reader, the dream he says, of a writing *naïve* and credulous.

> which by some immediate transfusion calls on the reader's belief as much as my own, from this dream, that has always existed in me, of another language, of a language entirely crude.
>
> (PERIOD I)

As if he could write without *him*, as if I could without being I write.

I shall stop here but it is essential to read the whole of this hallucinatory tale, the ruseful persecution of the Dream of naïveté, he is the dreamer philosopher, the only one, the martryr, the torn-between philosophy and naïveté, between faith and knowledge in which he *believes he knows* better than to believe, he who would like, who would really like to believe, but who believes he doesn't believe, what supreme naïveté, his, that of the dreamer of naïveté. He doesn't believe himself. Misfortune for him, fortunate for us. No one is less assured, no one more humble than he.

❖ ❖ ❖ ❖ ❖ ❖ ❖ ❖ ❖ ❖

From this first, blood-soaked period, I shall keep the word *relance* . . . and the vocable (he cannot say the word *word*) *cru* as in raw, crude, credulous . . . but we need to collect all of them, vein, transfusion, syringe, blood, sample, and into the bargain the words in the other language, Latin, the key words, dealt out with one hand even as they are being waved away by the other, drawn off into a language closed to many people, I recite, *cur confitemur Deo scienti* (Why confess to God, who is omniscient).

This book gives us the cure in Latin, a mother tongue said to be dead but his dearest wish is to resuscitate it (her) for us. I quote these words, I shall come back to them, to this *cur*, this why, it is the question and the response. I shall come back to it.

For the time being let us pursue him.

See him wondering [*se curir*] to himself, I mean running [*se courir*] after, pursuing himself, a runner on two tracks turning in opposite directions in this internal inadequacy that tears him apart, divorces him from himself, caught between I-don't-believe-so and I'd-like-to-believe-what-I-don't believe, torn, I say, but not decided. Divided, to his immense distress but not dogmatic, and hence not irreparable. Between him the subtle fabric of textuality tenders its thinking network, holding the lips of the wound together by means of signifying subterfuges. He tries to catch up with himself, he runs after himself he brings relief [*il se court après, il se court, il secourt*], he is the hero and thinker of the contretemps.

### The game of Circumfession

With the *vocable cru* and the *word relance* the game of circumfession begins.

We know, for he forewarned us, that as soon as it gets caught up in the writing the concept is cooked. So he tells himself. But how? How can he be both forewarned and forewarner? He begins, he'd like to have begun *before*, before himself, in the raw, before he gets caught up in it, and keep going faster and faster, hoping by sheer speed to outwit fatality. If one could put the *cru*, the crude, the raw, back into play, if there's any chance of that, he'll find it, he tells himself.

Note that from the first line we are therefore talking about overbidding [*relance*] not relief [*relève*]. Thanks to Georgette Esther.

—You've never played poker? he inquires, astonished.

I concede. A gap in my culture.

—In our house, I say, it was bridge. In our house, a household of German Jews who'd taken refuge in Algeria, there was a day for bridge, like the day for "Schabbat." Omi my grandmother, Rosi Klein, in her best silk to play bridge with Frau Hellman Frau Flörsheim Frau Morgenstern, and little cakes for tea in Dresden china.

—You were practically English, says he.

I admit it. Whereas poker is the mother's word. Poker, says he. I'm all ears, I say. And before my eyes poker asumes him like the Holy Ghost latching on to Elie and spiriting him off to heaven. Head up, I watch, I watch, it takes no time at all the assumption. I only had time to make note of what follows, the rest escaped me:

—Do you know what it means *to fan out your cards?* Poker he bellows (he's awfully high up already), I could play poker before I could read, you should have seen me! —I see you I shouted back. You should have seen me handle the cards, I could have been a pro in some Casino. I'll show you how to fan your cards. —Fan your cards, I say, dazzled! . . . —Look . . . If I haven't lost the knack says he. —Lost the knack! I shouted —You deal five cards to each player . . . You say give me three cards. You replace three cards.

—I replace I call dazzled.

—And when you get those cards you fan them out.

—I *fan them out?*

—You take the five cards in your left hand and with your right hand *very very gradually* you shuffle them around, you fold them, you twist them one behind the other, slide, gradually—gradually I say—so you can identify them by the first fraction of a millimeter . . . you make them appear—this maneuver takes time—as if you were unveiling, creating an absolutely extraordinary tension as you do.

We shuffle our cards around.

Bridge—bah—where are the blasts of wind, the torsions the torture, the taste for the pursuit of happiness?

—And so—the bidding, *la relance?* I prod.

—The bidding, it's *auction*, it's not English, it's poker.

I bid 1,000 francs. One thousand I say. If you want to bid higher, you say 1,500 francs.

The bid—or the bluff, *le bloff*—in my mother's mouth!

—Le bloff! Oh I know all about that. The bloff. It's Algero-Jewish colonist talk. You take the English words and dip them in honey. Le bloff my uncle used to say, le tob said Granny my Oran grandmother.

And to think I thought sheepishly, I thought I could more or less read him, I went to the mountain with my stick, accompanied by my name, along with Heidegger, Plato, Freud and the rest of them, but no poker, all my life I've missed out on poker, I blamed myself right up to the moment I began to think the contrary: all my life I've been playing poker without knowing it, I was in on the secret, and I was out of it. That's one shibboleth my mother never gave me.

To have as a mother someone whose passion is poker is not given to everyone. Even to him, she was nearly not given, or did not give herself as mother or for mother, because of this passion, as he tells it was told to him, in a short tale that his celerity as a professional player condenses to a sublime tragicomedy sublimely comical. Here's what they say about the birth of Jacques Derrida:

> from the same poker play in which I was born as they told me I was born, while *my mother, qualis illa erat, up to the last moment, that is my very birth*, in summer, in what in *El-Biar* they called a *villa, refused to interrupt at dawn a poker game*, the passion of her life, they say, her passion of life, and here among her last words, in the insensate flow I'm speaking

of, while amnesiac she no longer recognizes me or remembers my name, I hear her murmur, March 7, 1989, "I'm losing," then reply "I don't know" to the question "What does that mean?", and what I'm failing to translate here, under what death agony came to magnify in these words, is the almost quotidian tone of a verdict that I can still hear being said, "I'm losing," cards in hand, over there, on the other shore, in the middle of a poker game a summer's evening or just before the end.

(PERIOD 8)

Therefore the novel of this great thinker begins with the chapter preceding his birth, dashed off by mother-passion. For this scene as for his circumcision, he wasn't there, had he not been told about it he wouldn't be born, moreover his birth is a *last* moment, not a first, and there you have it, his birth put paid to his mother's game, there was no other moment aside from that one, already you can see the contretemps taking charge of his destiny, it's that my mother he says, *qualis illa erat, a i, i a, e a*, that's the way she was, but it's in Latin he says it a nice trick, upping it from the familiar to the noble, avoiding by means of recourse to the other language a tone of denunciation, quite the contrary, and then paying himself with the vowels of his name, *a e, a i, i a* all that happened in El-Biar *i a* in a villa *i a*, as for S. A. She refused to be interrupted, and he interrupted her. The Great Interrupter. In point of fact he very nearly remained inside Esther for the paradoxical reason of what he calls her passion of life. And now at the other end of time, in the final bed, at the last moment, the completely other, it is starting again, she no longer recognizes him, and, it seems to him, to him the son caught up in the contraband of love hate the mother initiated, it seems as though she's playing one last round, but invisible like god, this time, I'm losing she says.

But what had she said on the other side of the Mediterranean in Algeria, I wonder watching him play too in his race against time, afraid of not having finished before the last moment. What a pair they are, these two players whose aim is not to win, he insists vigorously but to go on playing up to and including the very last minute. She's a powerhouse his mother. And the best, it's that, as he tells us in period 39, one day at the age of eighty-five she goes for a swim between two poker games, can you beat that?

She enters the text now as the queen of *relance*, this word belongs to her he says, wily as he is, he grants her the *word*, the better to hold onto to the thing, don't you see.

And to prove to us on the spot that the supreme bidder, *the fastest gun*, is him, Elie, the man who makes drops and sparks gush from his speech, who can turn one word into twenty words, one sentence into a fabulous spate of philosophicoprophetical messages. A generalized eliquivocality. Listen to him throwing himself into the bidding for this diamond vocable, *cru*, from the start of the game, what a word, so big and so little, let's display it, let's fan it out, let's go after it, it's all over the place up it pops in every trick, there it is hiding in *quar*rel, you have to watch out for it, go after it.

> as though I were attached to him in order to look for a quarrel over what talking *cru*de means, as though I persisted, to the point of bloodshed, in reminding him, of what he knows, *cur confitemur Deo scienti* . . .

I go after him, I find *cur confitemur Deo scienti* there it is back again, and forever, *cur* is him as well, *why*, him. I follow the bidder who outbids his own flesh and blood like a superincarnate madman, he'd love to draw his chestnuts [*marrons*] from the flame he is, I meant his Marranos in his language, the other one, the one that has always been running after me—my language the other one—he says, running, I take his language the other one I keep *cru* as well—I'll come back to it—what is it he says above? *"only ever having loved the impossible"*—that's him in a nutshell, this confession, and this love, he loves everything that is the impossible, if he says that it is to light the way for us, for he is the poet and the prophet of the aporias that are our destiny and our

destination, he tells us because we don't want to tell ourselves, that's for sure
we say—but isn't it true, we too neither, we are unable to love anything but
the impossible, and similarly we can only forgive the unforgivable, he says it
over and over again, and if he repeats it, plays it anew in every text, raising
the stakes to body and soul, it's because it is one of those things we don't want
to know, the truth's logic we complain is impossible, it is cruel, it tries our
patience to the breaking point and yet and yet not only are we unable [*nous
impouvons*] but we have to be unable and similarly, following the example of
the knight of the impossible that he is, we can only *unbelieve*: *the believing {le
cru} in which I do not believe*, he says—it's incredible a phrase like that, how on
earth could they ever have translated it, with its pirouette on the word *cru*,
accruing in back of him—never having loved he says but that one belief the
one in which he doesn't believe, a *grand cru*, a fine wine from Algeria, vintage
Saint Augustine. "I don't believe." It fits him like a glove, fits the question of
his Judaism, this circumprofession of faith: saying the impossibility of opposing what's *cru*de and what's cooked, saying the crude neither crude nor creed,
not credible for him and therefore always already a little cooked up, licking
this word *cru* with his tongue inflamed with a searing love, this *cru*deness that
speaks of the flesh and ups the stakes to belief, this crossword, this crucible,
*cru* like incredible it is in it he believes he doesn't believe, doesn't believe he
believes, incredulous he caresses it, *cur, cur*, why, why he groans, can I not
believe you crude and nude, me and you. Why have I forsaken myself? Such
is his profession of faith in incredulity, always this quarrel looking to pick a
fight with itself at the heart of all believing.

You ask him: "Are you Jewish?" he responded: "I don't believe."

Let me say again, his language is untranslatable, whether or not there is
any believing, it cannot be that he does not believe in his own way, according to his personal faith, that he does not believe in what is nonetheless
believed, believed by others and perhaps believed for him, *except in his language*, that which pursues him and flees him, French foaming up sometimes

into its elder Latin. Raw belief [*le tout cru*], he tells us in French, I don't believe in it I dream of it. He discards the word and doesn't let go of it for he wants to split hairs by opposing—to whom—writing that's *naive*, that's his word and it's his name, raw [*tout cru*], newborn, not yet and never believed by anyone, writing to believe—one cannot believe the belief ready-made, to believe is in the present—writing that would be given to believe, to drink by transfusion, without delay. I don't believe I believe, he says. Which doesn't keep him from being credulous, yet another vein. Perhaps he believes in perhaps. It may be.

It's as though he dreamed of swimming, not between two rounds of poker like his mother, but between two temptations of incredulity, until he finds himself in sight of a believe.

In a poker match in French, this race between two circles, ruse and naïveté pursuing one another, he's had his share of luck, still you have to find the vein and draw on it, and immediately put it back in circulation as he does here, a real pro, see his dexterity, between commas, in the cutting up of a sentence, it's the luck of the draw, his lucky day, with the word *vein* in particular

and the word *cru* lets another vein flow into him through the ear canal, another stroke of luck, faith, profession of faith or confession, belief, credulity.

(PERIOD 1)

Syntactical amphibology, that's one motherlode—the luck of the ear canal another: faith a matter of luck, luck another name for grace, one may wish with all one's heart to have faith, having it depends neither on our desire nor on our will, as those who have it and those who don't have it know. Grace, a matter of chance—

But there are dreams, this marvelous ruse that saves us from faith from knowledge and from reason, from faith in knowledge and reason.

I shall only say a few words about this here: one does not enter the world of Confessions if one is not a *dreamer of* naïveté. They are, every one of them, *naïf*, they claim to be *naïf*, or to hope to be or to dream of being or to dream of ending up by being *naïf* Saint Augustine, Montaigne, Rousseau, Derrida, the one saying,

> I wish herein to be seen in my own simple, natural and ordinary fashion, without contention and artifice: for it is myself I portray. My faults will be read to the quick, and my form naive, so far as public reverence permits. For if I had been among those nations that they say still live under the sweet liberty of nature's first laws, I assure you I would most willingly have portrayed myself here in full, and wholly naked [*tout nud*] . . .

Saying

> Each man looks before himself; I look within myself: my business is only with myself, I consider myself constantly, I test myself, I taste myself. Others, if they think about it carefully, are always on their way elsewhere; they always go forward, as for me, I roll myself up into myself.
>
> This capacity for sorting out the truth, whatever it may be, within myself, and this free humour of mine, not readily to subjugate my beliefs, I owe principally to myself: for the firmest imaginations I have, and generalest, are those that, so to speak, were born with me. They are natural and wholly my own. I produced them crude [*crues*] and simple, by a hardy and strong production, but a little troubled and imperfect.

Saying, the other

> Here is the only portrait of a man, painted exactly from nature, and in all its truth, that exists and that will probably ever exist.

(Here I should deploy a chapter on the immense question of the unavowable, on the temptation of the avowal, on the avowal as temptation, of the Confessions all the "confessions," whether they be those of the saints or the criminals, as attempted avowal it's all the same, vain attempt. I should recall that the avowal or admission is always an attempt, *an essay*, and the essay always an admirable avowal, that is recognition of failure, the essay essays, and acknowledges itself as essay or avowal. The essay is *thought*, is this *exagium* that tells the weighing or pondering, hence the thought, the essay essays to think, attempts. The essay is attempted, as the avowal is tempted. To avow. There is temptation, one would like, with all one's strength, with all one's mind. Nothing is more tempting, tentative than the avowal. One wants one wants one wants, one can't. One wants that which one cannot want to desire. Want does not follow to be able does not follow want in the deadly corridors of the avowal. In any avowal, any dream of saying the worst, and only the worst is of interest to us, the presentiment—the desire and the fear, the desire-fear—of the unavowable murmurs. The avowal is always one of impotence. One can't. The avowal always vouches for its blindness [*l'aveu . . . se sait aveu-gle*]. The avowal is vowed to powerlessness. The avowal vows to keep the worst "in all its truth" unaltered. Here I should recall why we confess to God who knows, *cur confitemur Deo scienti*, why we only truly confess ourselves to God-who-knows because He knows it is not a question of knowing; and on condition: on condition there is no other witness than God-who-knows, on condition we make our confession to no one other than God, therefore to No One, to God-who-knows-as-likewise-He-does-not-know, to God the Ear for my word, God as my very own Ear into which, out my silence, I thrust my avowal, aloud, in order to hear myself and (not) be heard by anyone else (other than God). Not that I wish to cover my nakedness my sin my crime—so that they may be as if they didn't exist but quite the contrary so as to keep them fresh and fearful as at their dawning, intact, never attenuated. Here I should recall how Dostoyevsky (literature's most admirable sinner, excelling as no other at crime and at punishment that fails to punish) found the trick to keep the crime safe from punishment, for example, in *The Devils*, that Bible of Avowals. How he wrote so many hundreds of pages on the subject of Prince Stavrogin as one bandages and steel-plates a wound, how he kept it hidden, letting *the worst transpire* without ever saying it. How this thing that is in the throat of the character like a morsel of death that swells up till it chokes him never got spit out—not in the book, no, not in the room of the saintly man where the poor wretch came to *unavow*, to expire the worse. How the *unavowal* is kept out of the book close to the book in an extraordinary posthumous position. I am tempted by this chapter, but I renounce it for the time being in order to betake myself *to the scene of the Circumcision*.)

# V

## REMAIN/THE CHILD THAT I AM

*This is the story of Esther and the Rest of her*

The player who in the nick of time gives birth to him it is she who is first cause—there will be others—of his essential theme, the irresponsibility one might say initially overhastily for which she is not responsible she who didn't know his name, the sacred one, neither hers nor his, she who did not quote him, she who at the last moment, when he asked her "who am I?" did not answer him, she never was able to answer the question what am I, nor he either, like her, still today he asks *himself*. We mustn't skip over this slender scene. We need the mother's acknowledgment, she's the one we ask for the words, one word at least, *the* word Joyce said, the word that glues the pieces back together again. When she doesn't answer for me, I am broken. But how should she answer for a me? I am lodged in incapacity and there I remain, me on one hand my name on the other, the name calls me and who am I to answer? Here I remain, here I am a remains. The remains of Esther. The rest of Esther. Which would merely be a tragedy resonant with the note of abandonment had it not in this case become the most powerful philosophy.

Mummy did not leave him his (her) letters. She left him this forsakingness and all the rest of her constant distraction, all the rest this indecipherable, evasive mother, who keeps her secret right up to death the loser who loses the other, even as she is at the origin of the undecidable, which sounds like something Derrida might say. She remains to him, in leaving, after her departure, like those questions without response that come back to haunt us. She remains with her questioning name. *Es-ther? Est-ce taire?*

About filiation and its consequences—which counts a lot in Judaism you know how they say: the Derrida son, the Cixous daughter—he knows everything, how paradoxically it controls ex/dis/appropriation within the family, the inadequacy, the structural dissociation of the subject—he who says *moi* in French, this self that I am not and that speaks more loudly than I, "*qui je suis—moi* [who am I—me]?" knowing all along that one will never know he should so like to know. And, in the meantime, *reste que je suis: (it/the) remains that I am,* he who is the rest or the remains of Esther, and he who remains, *rests,* but restless, relief but without *relief.* The rest of Esther is silence, metonymy, he is an infinite restingness and will remain forever a child, the only one who so remains including plumb in the middle of the gravest philosophical symposia, and more precisely he remains the child *que* [*that*]. *Que,* his inseparable, another untranslatable vocable *que,* that we saw make its appearance in Jacques. *Que* around which he turns idiomatically each time he wants to accede to a one-self. Who? The child *that* I am he says in *Voiles;* that is the animal *that* I am in other words "the intercessor *that* I am, you, Elie, I call upon you intercede for me . . . Elie, I'm calling you, break down the barriers, intercede for the intercessor *that* I am, you, for the third circumcision before the first . . . " *That* I am. One might say a sort of relative, epithet, or attribute, and what is an epithet that tells the essence? Tells also what I am not. Tells also that *I am not there, in the child,* not contained, I am not that child in *itself* "the child *that* the grown-ups enjoyed reducing to tears . . . who was always to weep over himself with the mother's tears. . . . I am sorry *for myself,* I'm crying *over myself* . . . but like *another,* another wept over by another weeper. . . . I weep from my mother over the child *whose substitute I am* whence the other, nongrammatical syntax that remains to be invented to speak of the name of God, etc." (period 23).

That's the key: this *like* or *as if*. I am *as if* I were another. He is as if, like (as if he were) another. True, we are all substitutes, but he is a substitute truly like no-one. He writes books that are *like* books [*comme des livres*]. *As if* delivered [*comme délivrés*]. Such substitutingness haunts him, to be conscious of this as-if-being is to suffer, but it is also the condition of wisdom: an antidote for our presumption. Whereupon the child *that* I am, the animal that, the remains that, the satyr galatea that I am, the Jew that I am, enjoys the privileges of idiomatic homonymy: the child *that I am* (*that I follow*), if I am it (if I follow it), it is that I am in the place from which I observe it, I can only follow it if I am not it, I am not the one that I am (that I follow), do you follow me? O my imi gration my grace.

This child, therefore, is not him, it is not the child, it is not a child, the same one, he is not a child but there is one in him, ready to cry, to shed tears, saliva, feminine sperm, masculine drool while apparently holding back his tears, in truth he doesn't know it but he gets news of it from time to time, I feel that I carry it around with me he says in *La Contre-Allée* (like a child in my belly, I can hear its heart) he moves around with it like a secret. *A secret at work* that does not stop secreting itself and secreting him and moving him from within. His password is *comme*: *like* and *as*.

Should you want a photo of him, as they used to say in Algeria, you would find it in *Voiles*: he filmed himself as a silkworm, a little Jewish, a little Algerian, a little amphisexual. A silk worm weaver, a spinner (male and female), comparable to a scroll of the Torah, the autobiography of the lure says he, one can read lure-autobiography, that of all his selves, me or he or she or thee, and the rest of the unconscious guests.

How beautiful it is, the childhood memory in question, the worm, which is a sex that is not a sex, dead and self-entombed he is not dead, and he is truly the only one to have managed to put sericircumcision in place of circumcision, a simulacrum of death with resurrection that plays on a miraculous penis with feminine ejaculation, the *rev-{ver}-erie* of resurrection.

Being an as if I were another who am I to say that I am Jewish, that is the question he tracks like a hunter.

I shall keep Like and As If [*Comme et Si*] for later. And linger a moment on an other that he particularly does not wish to be reduced to being, in his logic of being faithful to substitution, and this is: *a point, a dot*. Among his fears he has one fear "*that of the writer who fears dying* before the end of a long sentence, *period* [*un point c'est tout*]" (period 10). To die as a point or a period or a full stop would be terrible. Full-stop-end-of-sentence should be written as a single word, another of those idiomatic tags that torment the translator. Just imagine, instead of a sentence as long as the world, to have been nothing but a fullstopendofsentence, a writer who's nothing but a dot, a point, a dot dot, nothing left over, a dot without its I! just imagine, a foreskin without its penis in sum, but that's just fantasy, and which shows us precisely what Jacques Derrida dreads: the point the one nail capable of crucifying the silk worm. Cruel crucipuncture.

How right he is to fear dying and that she die. His mother. The author of his days and (of) his writing.

## The writing that speaks for whom

Who speaks for whom, period 4 asks: "Consign them here, but why I wonder, confide to the bottom of this book what were the last more or less intelligible sentences of my mother, still alive at the moment I am writing this." I wanted to study the time of the mother, but that doesn't mean anything, the time of the mother still alive, but that doesn't mean anything either, I should say: the time of the mother is always the time of the mother still alive. That is, I disrupt slightly the temporality of my own thoughts, the time of

the mother is always the time of the life, it is the time of life's origin, as
Ferenczi said, of sexual life, one could double this up and say that the mother's time is always the time of the origin of sexual life. What *Circumfession* says
is that: the labor with the mother on the edge of the mother around the
mother, turnng around the bed, staying close to her shore, is a labor on and
with sexuality. Therefore it is the time of the origin of sexual life, and the
time of the end: we all live because the mother inscribes the beginning and
the end for us, not taking milestones into account, not taking boundaries and
limits into account. One cannot not take the dates of birth and death into
account but the mother overflows these banks, we are in her, she is in us;
wherever the period falls, infinity remains. This is what the son has inscribed
in this period with its work on verb tenses. His texts are haunted by enallage,
a figure that consists in slightly displacing the notes of the scale, and in a
poignant manner, in the verbal scale, in the tenses of the verbs. I listen to him
accommodating himself to the torment of not understanding himself:

"Consign them here, but why I ask, confide to the bottom of this book
what *were* the last more or less intelligible sentences of my mother, still alive
at the moment I *am writing* this" (my emphasis).

Equivocation and enallage introduce first a past then a present into this
moment, into this period. In this manner he's going to circumnavigate within the time of the mother or within the mother. Addressing himself and
dividing himself so as to ask (himself) (whom?) not *why confide*—but why
confide *to the bottom* of the book—no, not to ask why/confide/to the bottom/
but *why* ask himself what he is asking—no, that's not the question, the question is why deposit still living sentences in the soil or ground of the book,
thereby consigning them and cosigning them, a funereal gesture of circon-
servation. How to say the expression "still living," if not by counting back
time from the moment of death? For indeed writing is a sort of turning back
time, telling us that time can be disoriented, that it can go both ways. As if
it were always at the same age younger and older than itself. Which also

inscribes the moment of telling myself: she is still alive. I catch myself, why say she is still alive? That rings in different ways, it rings the alarm, it rings with fear, it has also a ring of triumph, I could say "always still alive." Similarly I could say life is "always-still," furthermore that we only feel the preciousness and the reality of life in relation to nonlife. We receive life only from death. We only have it, only feel it, only live it from the wrong side out, which makes it a sort of porosity, never the one without the other, which makes life an in-mourning but also gives us serenity in the face of death, everything being at the disposition of the subject who undertakes this circumnavigation within without, safeguarding and within the still. At this point he deliberately exaggerates as to her last sentences, as if she were already dead still alive, which terms can be inversed she is still alive though dead already; and him too. A scene for two, two whom one can neither separate nor oppose, since they are each for the other part of each other. When can one say: "the last sentences" or "still alive"? Here it seems to him that this still living mother is no longer. So he says, *a little lower*, very, very low, one can no longer even hear him: "and I am writing here at the moment my mother no longer recognizes me, and at which she no longer calls me, and for her, for the rest of her life, I no longer have a name." At this moment, the place of the still living, the in one's lifetime, begins to appear mobile. If his mother no longer calls him, he is no longer called. The experience we have of death in life when it is not linked to the disappearance of someone by death but to their being in suspense, is there: she no longer calls me, I can call her, she no longer calls me. Half the way or half the life remains: Without sound without echo. She no longer says my name. My name no longer exists either. Death is within me, it is not the dead person who is dead, it is I who am the bearer of her death. One shares the death as one shares the life. Furthermore, this death or this life are also divided, the life by the death, or the death by the life. We are exhausted, emptied out.

This is what is said here in tones of mourning without violence and with the help of enallages of tense such that period 4 flows strangely between its past and its present, a past that is introduced in the present as a future past, as the past that approaches "without my knowing henceforth any more clearly myself who will have asked her such and such a question like the other day in Nice." I don't know where he is either, sometimes he's in Nice, sometimes he is not in Nice but he is writing of Nice. Time is written in space: "the other day in Nice when I asked her if she was in pain ('yes')," this quotation set off from the rest of the phrase, hers or his, the yes is kept locked up cut off with a double bolt from the person who pronounced it. A yes may alight on one or the other shore. "Then where, it was February 5, 1989, she had, in a rhetoric that could never have been hers, the audacity of this stroke about which she will, alas, never know anything, no doubt knew nothing, and that piercing the night replies to my question." "*She had,*" "*replies,*" from a preterite to a present. "I have a pain in my mother." The *question* is perhaps also that of the first line: "why *I ask*" "as though she were speaking *for* me," both in my direction, she speaks toward me and in place of me. In other words: "I have a pain in my mother" is a sentence of his for him, as when he says in the beginning "the more or less intelligible sentences of my mother [*les phrases . . . intelligibles de ma mère*]," which in the French construction can also be his own sentences, his own sentences intelligible for my mother. "I have a pain in my mother," the sentence complains: where does it it hurt? it hurts in my mother. In my mother as in my stomach, in my throat, in some part of me. As she is part of him, he is a part of her.

And I hear myself use the word *part,* which belongs to the semantics of departure, of partition.

"Although in the apparently amnesiac confusion in which she is ending/ she ended [*elle finit*] her days," here we have a play on *finir* brought about by the phonic coincidence in French of past and present tense—

"The memory of her mother, her own mother, is so very present to her" she forgets but she remembers her mother, she forgets but her mother remembers for her, her so very present mother. He adds "her own mother" as though it might be unclear, but the confusion can only be his. Because she is a part of him and he is a part of her. The amnesiac muddles, they are him too.

"That she looks more and more like, I mean like my grandmother." He cuts the family pack of cards, he shuffles them so rapidly the changes are dizzying, even to the point of Freudian slips.

Same problem with the attribution, this time of place: "then on the evening of the same day, when she was alone with me in that house, and I was in a different room," the other day, the other room, "several times in a row she had exposed herself naked after frantically pulling off the clothes that were hampering her in her bed." Who then saw her naked? It needs a logical enallage, one can always say that he must have come back to the room, but he wrote that he is in *another room*. And he states that he is alone with her in the house. The naked exposition can only have no one as witness, him as other, herself etc. Is there some lack of care in this great wave of a sentence, which results in a kind of awkwardness, a strangeness that is not part of the conscious plan? This carelessness is deliberate, this lack of control of the limits that means the other-room is the same room, a memory occupies the amnesia room. The improbable here shows what it is capable of. No one to say the contrary. One is in place of the other.

Here is therefore next door, there is also here. Same continuity, simultaneity coalescence of the times of Time, as though there were only one time with ephemeral sighs, 1977 respires in 1989, feebly but still, everything can call itself future, future perfect for the one who declares—will have declared—"I posthume as I breathe" brilliantly inventing the verb to posthume, for his own personal usage as a "survivor" who wants to make liars of life and death. There you have him then he who dies at the top of his lungs, a buried-alive supernatural, who gets wind of a new definition of immortali-

**16** Elle devient à présent, je suis près d'elle ce 18 juin, ce que toujours elle fut, l'impassibilité d'un temps hors du temps, une mortelle immortelle, trop humaine inhumaine, le dieu muet la bête, une eau dormante au fond désormais apaisé de l'abîme, ce volcan dont je me dis que je me suis bien sorti, *in istam dico uitam mortalem, an mortem uitalem, ? nescio,* elle bouge peu sur son lit, les doigts seulement, elle regarde sans voir, entend à peine et comme « les analyses sont bonnes », qu'elle « mange et dort bien », ce qui lui reste d'avenir, indéfiniment dirait-on car on ne peut plus compter, sur elle ni en quoi que ce soit et c'est donc la vraie vie, sa vie donc rassure et inquiète les autres, les siens, au seul signe d'évolution qui ait encore couleur de désir, d'histoire ou d'événement, autrement dit le sang, s'appelant d'un nom que j'apprends à apprendre, de fond en comble, l'*escarre*, un archipel de volcans rouges et noirâtres, plaies enflammées, croûtes et cratères, des signifiants en puits profonds de plusieurs centimètres, s'ouvrant ici, se fermant là, sur les talons, les hanches et le sacrum, la chair même exhibée en son dedans, plus de secret, plus de peau, mais elle paraît ne pas souffrir, elle ne les voit pas comme moi au moment où l'infirmière dit « ils sont beaux » pour marquer que leur être-à- vif, le caractère encore non nécrosé du tissu laisse espérer une cicatrisation, et j'essaie de la faire parler. « Qu'est-ce que tu me dis ? – Je sais pas. – ... – Quoi ? », ou « Qu'est-ce que tu me racontes ? – Qu'est-ce que je raconte ? – Oui. – Rien », mais elle répond mieux au téléphone, dont le dispositif revient à faire sombrer le monde pour laisser le passage de la voix pure vers le fond de la mémoire, et c'est ainsi qu'il y a peu elle a prononcé mon nom, Jackie, en écho à la phrase de ma sœur qui lui passait l'écouteur, « bonjour Jackie », ce qu'elle n'avait pu faire depuis des mois et ne fera peut-être plus, outre qu'elle sut à peine, au long de sa vie, l'autre nom : « *Élie : mon nom – non inscrit, le seul, très abstrait, qui me soit arrivé, que j'ai appris, du dehors, plus tard, et que je n'ai jamais senti, porté, le nom que je ne connais pas, c'est comme un numéro (mais lequel ! matricule allais-je dire en pensant à la plaque de l'Élie mort que porte Marguerite ou au suicide, en 1955, de mon ami Élie Carrive) désignant anonymement le nom caché, et en ce sens, plus que tout autre, c'est le nom donné, que j'ai reçu sans le recevoir là où ce qui est reçu ne doit pas se recevoir, ni donner aucun signe de reconnaissance en échange (le nom, le don), mais dès que j'ai appris, très tard, que c'était mon nom, j'y ai placé, très distraitement, mis de côté, en réserve, une certaine noblesse, un signe d'élection, je suis celui qu'on élit, ceci joint à l'histoire du thaleth blanc (à raconter ailleurs) et à quelques autres signes de bénédiction secrète* » (23-12-76), mon escarre même.

**10** Aléa ou arbitraire du point de départ, l'irresponsabilité même direz-vous, l'incapacité où je demeure de répondre de mon nom, de le rendre même à ma mère, reste que je suis ici, maintenant, supposons-le, car jamais je ne pourrai le démontrer, le contre-exemple en série de ce que j'ai jamais pu écrire ou de ce que G. peut en savoir, et la peur qui me tient depuis toujours, car à cela du moins je suis fidèle, se désaccorde, elle se menace depuis deux imminences apparemment contradictoires, celle de l'écrivain qui craint de mourir avant la fin d'une longue phrase, un point c'est tout, sans signer le contre-exemple, et celle du fils qui, redoutant de la voir mourir avant la fin de l'aveu, pour cette confession promise à la mort, tremble donc aussi de partir avant sa mère, cette figure de la survivance absolue dont il a tant parlé, mais aussi celle qui ne pourrait à la lettre le pleurer, ce serait excès de souffrance pour qui a déjà perdu deux fils, l'un avant moi, Paul Moïse, mort en 1929 à moins d'un an, un an avant ma naissance, ce qui dut faire de moi pour elle, pour eux, un précieux mais si vulnérable intrus, un mortel de trop, Élie aimé à la place d'un autre, puis l'autre après moi, Norbert Pinhas, mort à deux ans alors que j'en avais dix, en 1940, sans la moindre image de sa circoncision que pourtant je me rappelle, et je vis alors le premier deuil comme le deuil de ma mère qui ne pourrait donc à la lettre me pleurer, moi le seul remplaçant, me pleurer comme le devront mes fils, alors que mon seul désir reste de donner à lire l'interruption qui de toute façon décidera de la figure même, cette écriture ressemblant à la pauvre chance d'une résurrection provisoire, comme celle qui eut lieu en décembre 1988 quand un coup de téléphone de mon beau-frère me précipita vers le premier avion pour Nice, cravate, costume sombre, *kippa* blanche dans la poche, essayant en vain non seulement de pleurer mais je ne sais plus, de m'empêcher de pleurer, *et fletum frenabam*, de me soustraire à tous les programmes et à toutes les citations, quand l'imprévisible ne manqua pas de se produire, me surprenant absolument mais comme ce qui va de soi, l'inflexible destin, à savoir qu'incapable le soir de me reconnaître et devant au dire des médecins ne survivre que quelques heures, voici qu'au petit matin, à l'instant où, ayant dormi seul chez elle, j'arrivai le premier dans la chambre blanche de la clinique, elle me vit, m'entendit et revint, pour ainsi dire, à elle, comme immortelle, sA en fit aussi l'expérience, il en eut, il en fut le savoir Absolu, sA le raconte, *cito reddita est sensui*, et j'écris entre deux résurrections, la donnée puis la promise, compromise à ce monument presque naturel qui devient à mes yeux une sorte de racine calcinée, le spectacle nu d'une blessure photographiée – l'escarre cautérisée par la lumière de l'écriture, à feu, à sang mais à cendre aussi.

Les lits secrets d'Élie
ou l'hypothèse

**17** Plongé dans l'histoire de la pénitence, du repentir au regret et à la contrition, de l'aveu public avec expiation à l'aveu privé et à la confession, de la réconciliation publique à la réparation puis à l'absolution, entre le sang et l'eau, et le baptême, et les voiles blancs et rouges, Tertullien l'Africain, le concile de Latran et saint Jean Népomucène, martyr du secret de la confession, et saint Augustin dont je lis que « revenu à Dieu, il ne s'est probablement jamais confessé, au sens moderne du mot », n'ayant jamais eu, pas plus que moi, au-delà même de la vérité, « l'occasion de "se confesser" », ce qui ne l'empêche justement pas de travailler à l'accouchement des confessions littéraires, soit à une forme de théologie comme autobiographie, je me demande, moi que n'intéressent au fond de l'escarre ni l'écriture ni la littérature, ni l'art, ni la philosophie, ni la science, ni la religion, ni la politique, seulement la mémoire et le cœur, non pas même l'histoire de la présence du présent, je me demande ce que je cherche avec cet aveu à la machine, au-delà des institutions, la psychanalyse comprise, au-delà du savoir de la vérité, qui n'a rien à voir ici, au-delà même de l'hypothèse « scandaleusement belle » de mon nom secret, Élie, autour duquel tournaient les premiers carnets de 1976, des carnets de dessin à feuilles épaisses dont la couverture portait une escarre, c'est-à-dire un blason à deux lions donnant à lire en bordure d'un carré ouvert les mots *skizze, croquis, sketch, schizzo, schets, kpoki,* et j'y ajoutais à la main, en hébreu, le mot pour mot, מִילָה, prononcez *milah,* qui nomme le mot et la circoncision, cherchant à savoir déjà qui au fond Élie aurait aimé, de qui, « dernier visage aimé », il eût choisi de recevoir son nom comme une absolution au terme d'une confession sans vérité, pour l'amour de toi, pour faire l'amour de toi, pour faire ce que je fais ici par l'amour que tu porterais à Élie, *amore amoris tui facio istuc,* ainsi « *le fait que ce prénom n'ait pas été inscrit [à l'état civil comme le furent les noms hébreux de ma famille] (comme si on avait voulu le cacher, plus encore que les autres noms hébreux, placés après les autres), ait été comme effacé, retenu, signifiait plusieurs choses mêlées : d'abord qu'on voulait me cacher comme un prince dont on dissimule provisoirement la filiation pour le garder en vie (je pense à l'instant, cherchant à m'expliquer ce geste (dont mes parents ne m'ont jamais parlé, au sujet duquel je ne les ai jamais interrogés, cela restant secondaire et n'occupant tant de place ici qu'en raison du fil que j'ai choisi de suivre) qu'un frère mourut à quelques mois, moins d'un an avant ma naissance, entre mon frère aîné, René [Abraham], et moi. Il s'appelait Paul Moïse), le garder en vie jusqu'au jour où sa royauté pourrait [...] s'exercer au grand jour, sans risque pour la précieuse semence ; ensuite que je devais ne pas porter au jour de signe juif* » (23-12-76).

l'histoire
li
li li
ile lie
secret
lis li il

il li

littérature
philosophie
religion
politique
sca
secret sc
escarre
sk

il li l'i

sec

**8** Comme si je n'aimais que ta mémoire et confession de moi mais qui serais-je, moi, si je ne commençais et finissais par t'aimer, toi, dans ma langue privée de toi, celle-là même, l'intraduisible, où le bon mot nous laisse à terre, gagnants et perdants comme le jour où une préméditation de l'amour m'avait dicté pour l'immortalité, non, pour la postérité, non, pour la vérité que tu es, *et lex tua ueritas, et ueritas tu*, « n'oublie pas que je t'aurai aimé », me croyant alors assez malin pour éviter le conditionnel en précisant à voix si haute « A I, bien sûr », Jackie, les voyelles, ma voix de ton nom ou du nom de mon unique sœur, et ne percevant qu'après coup cette avance même ou ce retard par lesquels une haine s'efface en contrebande pour s'échanger avec l'amour de toi, avec le don de moi, *ego uero cogitans dona tua, deus* invisibilis, du même coup de poker où je suis né, comme on m'a dit que je suis né, alors que ma mère, *qualis illa erat,* jusqu'au dernier moment, à savoir ma naissance même, l'été, dans ce qu'on appelait à El-Biar une villa, refusa d'interrompre à l'aube une partie de poker, la passion de sa vie, disent-ils, sa passion de la vie, et voici que parmi ses dernières paroles, dans le flux insensé dont je parle, alors qu'amnésique elle ne me reconnaît plus ni ne se rappelle mon nom, je l'entends murmurer, le 7 mars 1989, « je suis perdante », puis répondre « je ne sais pas » à la question « qu'est-ce que ça veut dire ? », et ce que j'échoue à traduire ici, sous ce que l'agonie venait magnifier en ces mots, c'est le ton quasiment quotidien d'un verdict que je l'entends encore prononcer, « je suis perdante », les cartes à la main, là-bas, sur l'autre rive, en pleine partie de poker un soir d'été ou juste avant la fin, celle après laquelle je cours, me demandant à chaque instant si elle vivra encore, ayant toutefois cessé de me connaître, quand j'arriverai au bout de cette phrase qui semble porter la mort qui la porte, si elle vivra assez pour me laisser le temps de tous ces aveux, et de multiplier les scènes où je me vois seul mourir, prier, pleurer, au terme d'une circumnavigation qui cherche à s'arriver dans une histoire de sang, là où je suis enfin ce nom cautérisé, l'ultime, l'unique, tout contre ce que j'ai, depuis une circoncision improbable, perdu en le gagnant, et quand je dis que je veux contre G. gagner mon nom, cela ne veut pas dire le contraire de perdre, que l'on entende gagner au sens du jeu, gagner au poker, ou au sens du voyage, gagner la rive, ou au sens du labeur, gagner sa vie, l'horrible mot que *je gagne,* voilà ce qu'ils n'auront jamais compris, je n'aime ni le mot ni la chose, d'où le renvoi indéfini, ladite théologie négative, le jeu avec les noms de Dieu, la substitution d'une rive à l'autre, la panique hémophile qui s'interrompt à l'ordre venu d'en haut et d'en face à la fois, l'injonction rythmée à laquelle sans me faire prier je cède.

# Le cru et le cur

**1** Le vocable cru, lui disputer ainsi le cru, comme si d'abord j'aimais à le relancer, et le mot de « relance », le coup de poker n'appartient qu'à ma mère, comme si je tenais à lui pour lui chercher querelle quant à ce que parler cru veut dire, comme si jusqu'au sang je m'acharnais à lui rappeler, car il le sait, *cur confitemur Deo scienti,* ce qui nous est par le cru demandé, le faisant ainsi dans ma langue, l'autre, celle qui depuis toujours me court après, tournant en rond autour de moi, une circonférence qui me lèche d'une flamme et que j'essaie à mon tour de circonvenir, n'ayant jamais aimé que l'impossible, le cru auquel je ne crois pas, et le mot cru laisse affluer en lui par le canal de l'oreille, une veine encore, la foi, la profession de foi ou la confession, la croyance, la crédulité, comme si je tenais à lui pour lui chercher dispute en opposant un écrit naïf, crédule, qui par quelque transfusion immédiate en appelle à la croyance du lecteur autant qu'à la mienne, depuis ce rêve en moi depuis toujours d'une autre langue, d'une langue toute crue, d'un nom à demi fluide aussi, là, comme le sang, et j'entends ricaner, pauvre vieux, t'en prends pas le chemin, c'est pas demain la veille, tu sauras jamais, la surabondance d'une crue après le passage de laquelle une digue devient belle comme la ruine qu'elle aura toujours au fond d'elle-même emmurée, la cruauté surtout, encore le sang, *cruor, confiteor,* ce que le sang aura été pour moi, je me demande si Geoff le sait, comment saurait-il que ce matin-là, un 29 novembre 1988, telle phrase est venue, de plus loin que je ne saurai jamais dire, mais une seule phrase, à peine une phrase, le mot pluriel d'un désir vers lequel tous les autres depuis toujours semblaient, la confluence même, se presser, un ordre suspendu à trois mots, *trouver la veine,* ce qu'un infirmier pouvait murmurer, une seringue à la main, la pointe dressée vers le haut, avant la *prise de sang,* lorsque par exemple dans mon enfance, et je me rappelle ce laboratoire dans une rue d'Alger, la peur et la vague d'un glorieux apaisement s'emparaient à la fois de moi, me prenaient aveugle dans leurs bras à l'instant précis où par la pointe de la seringue s'assurait un passage invisible, toujours invisible, pour l'écoulement continu du sang, absolu, absous en ce sens que rien ne semblait s'interposer entre la source et l'embouchure, le dispositif assez compliqué de la seringue n'étant introduit à cette place que pour laisser le passage et disparaître en tant qu'instrument, mais continu en cet autre sens que, sans l'intervention maintenant brutale de l'autre qui, décidant d'interrompre le flot une fois la seringue, toujours dressée, retirée du corps, repliait vivement mon bras vers le haut et pressait le coton à l'intérieur du coude, le sang eût pu inonder encore, non pas indéfiniment mais continûment jusqu'à m'épuiser, aspirant ainsi vers lui ce que j'appelai : le glorieux apaisement.

*[marginal handwritten notes:]*
lui qui ?
qui lui ?
lui ?
le mot cru ?
elle ?
ma mère ?
ou Dieu ?
ou bien
lui ?

ou elle ?

ou bien
c'est lui
le sang
qui aura
lui ?

**18** L'escarre, ô ma jalousie, et tant que je ne t'aurai pas comprise, à savoir suturée, ô ma jalousie, comme escarre se referme sur le sang à se refaire la peau, tant que je ne saurai pas d'où tu viens exploser, ma jalousie, d'où tu exposes le dedans de la brûlure à vif de mon corps au pire, le tordant de douleur comme ce visage qui depuis trois jours (28-6-89) se paralyse en une hideuse grimace, la grimace de ma lucidité, l'œil gauche ouvert et fixe sous l'effet d'un virus dont je concluais il y a quelques mois, rappelant que le virus aura été le seul objet de mon travail, « le virus n'a pas d'âge », et je parlais du virus du computer aussi bien que du sida, tant que je n'aurai pas écrit un traité *marquant* l'origine et la fin de ma jalousie, *De l'indubitable fondement ou le cogito de ma jalousie,* ou encore *Les Confessions d'une mère,* j'aurai manqué ma vie et n'aurai rien écrit, adieu le salut, paralysie faciale incurable, masque, hypocrisie, parjure insondable, lunettes noires, eau qui retombe de la bouche, colère d'infirme, multiplication des escarres sur le corps de la mère comme sur le mien, de la chose et des mots, j'aime trop les mots parce que je n'ai pas de langue à moi, seulement de fausses escarres, de faux foyers *(eskhara),* ces croûtes noirâtres et purulentes qui se forment autour des plaies sur le corps de ma mère, sous les talons, puis sur le sacrum et sur les hanches, nombreuses, vivantes, grouillantes d'homonymies, toutes ces escarres, foyers d'autel pour dieux et sacrifices, brasier, feu de bivouac, sexe de la femme, l'escharose du mot lui-même engendrant une énorme famille de bâtards étymologiques, de progénitures qui changent de nom et dont l'escarre homonyme, l'équerre du blason quarré, donne lieu aux généalogies en abîme dont je n'abuserai pas mais je ne m'arrête pas ici sans noter le lien avec la cicatrice anglaise, *scar,* ou avec la coupure du haut-allemand, *scar,* l'eschatologie de ma circoncision, car ce terme vieilli, l'escarre venu de *scar,* signifie l'éclat, la violence de l'effraction par avant-garde (car au-delà de tous les usages vieillis de ce mot de passe, ils ne m'ont jamais pardonné d'être l'eschatologiste le plus avancé, la dernière avant-garde qui compte, car l'escart, un autre mot, dit l'avance de l'écolier sur l'adversaire au jeu des barres), si je meurs avant ma mère, ou G., *nam etsi descendero in infernum, ades,* aurai-je pris de l'avance à mourir ou à survivre, toujours à faire faux bond car *« je ne leur appartenais plus du jour de ma naissance, cela lié à ce double sentiment qui m'a toujours précédé : j'étais à la fois exclu et infiniment, secrètement préféré par ma famille qui m'avait perdu, dès l'origine, par amour, d'où une série de ruptures sans rupture avec elle, l'impossibilité assurée dès le départ du mariage endogame et finalement, après le débat qu'il faut raconter, la non-circoncision de mes fils. Le prophète Élie est pourtant le gardien de la circoncision »* (23-12-76) ?

Signé : *l'escharretiste de la fin*

**14** Par exemple, et je date, c'est la première page des carnets, « *Circoncision, je n'ai jamais parlé que de ça*, considérez le discours sur la limite, les marges, marques, marches, etc., la clôture, l'anneau (alliance et don), le *sacrifice*, l'écriture du corps, le pharmakos exclu ou retranché, la coupure / couture de Glas, le coup et le recoudre, d'où l'hypothèse selon laquelle c'est de ça la circoncision, que, sans le savoir, en n'en parlant jamais ou en parlant au passage, comme d'un exemple, je parlais ou me laissais parler toujours, à moins que, autre hypothèse, la circoncision elle-même ne soit qu'un exemple de ça dont je parlais, oui mais j'ai été, je suis et je serai toujours, moi et non un autre, circoncis, et il y a là une région qui n'est plus d'exemple, c'est elle qui m'intéresse et me dit non pas comment je suis un cas mais où je ne suis plus un cas, quand le mot d'abord, au moins, CIRCONCIS, à travers tant et tant de relais, multipliés par ma "culture", le latin, la philosophie, etc., tel qu'il s'est imprimé dans ma langue à son tour circoncise, n'a pas pu ne pas travailler, tirer en arrière, de tous les côtés, aimer, oui, un mot, milah, en aime un autre, tout le lexique qui obsède mes écrits, CIR-CON-SI, s'imprime dans l'hypothèse de la cire, non, ça c'est faux et mauvais, pourquoi, qu'est-ce qui ne marche pas, mais scie, oui, et tous les points sur les i, j'y ai beaucoup insisté ailleurs, Mallarmé, Ponge, mais c'était bien de cela que je parlais, le point détaché et retenu en même temps, la fausse, non pas fausse mais simulée castration qui ne perd pas ce qu'elle joue à perdre et qui le transforme en lettre prononçable, i et non pas I, puis tenir toujours le plus grand compte, dans l'anamnèse, de ce fait que dans ma famille et chez les Juifs d'Algérie, on ne disait presque jamais la "circoncision" mais le "baptême", non la Bar Mitzwa mais "la communion", avec les conséquences de l'adoucissement, de l'affadissement, par acculturation apeurée, dont j'ai toujours souffert plus ou moins consciemment, d'événements inavouables, ressentis comme tels, pas "catholiques", violents, barbares, durs, "arabes", circoncision circoncise, accusation de meurtre rituel intériorisée, secrètement assumée » (20-12-76), le temps cité de ce carnet tire le fil blanc d'une période recoupant les trois autres, au moins, 1. le théologiciel de sA, 2. le savoir absolu ou géologiciel de G. comme 3. la survie présentement présente ou vie par provision de Georgette Sultana Esther, si vous préférez Maman, qui recoupe tout, synchronie risquant de cacher l'essentiel, à savoir que la confession retenue n'aura pas été de ma faute mais de la sienne, comme si la fille de Zipporah n'avait pas seulement commis le crime de ma circoncision mais un autre encore, plus tard, le premier jouant le coup d'envoi, le péché originel contre moi, mais pour se reproduire et m'acharner, me mettre à la question, moi, une vie entière, pour la faire avouer, elle, en moi.

ça  cir
ça
sac- ice
ça  cir
ïs
cas

cir  cas
cir
cir
xi
ça
mais scie
mais si
ça
cas
ïs
ci
sci
cir
ti
cit
ciel
si  zi!
ïs
ti ti

ô mon homohéliesexualité impossible!

**31** « *Son amour a raison de moi, ai-je écrit cette phrase pour sa valeur, son sens, sa vérité, son actualité, ou parce que, dans ses pouvoirs syntaxiques et lexicaux, elle comporte un potentiel économique formidablement formalisé, rendue d'avance là où ça saigne, et combien d'énoncés de ce type ai-je laissé se perdre, faute de surface d'inscription immédiatement disponible, sans savoir s'ils s'inscrivaient ailleurs, ni ce qui reste une fois la surface d'inscription enterrée, comme le foreskin ou la moleskine... coin of a new concept, fellocirconcision, auto-fellocirconcision, le mohel de soi-même plié en deux, de mon rire, après avoir pris, et gardé, une gorgée de vin dans sa bouche, du rosé d'Algérie très frais, on en buvait à la pêcherie, il se circoncit, la "lyre" dans une main, le couteau dans l'autre, et boit son propre sang, pour se rendre encore plus propre, c'est-à-dire circoncis, il se dit alors je t'aime et dans l'ivresse se met à pleurer sa solitude, mon amour aura eu raison de moi* » (31-12-76), selon ce qu'il faut bien déclarer, comme à la douane, mon homosexualité impossible, celle que j'associerai toujours au nom de Claude, les cousins-cousines de mon enfance, ils débordent mon corpus, la syllabe CL, dans *Glas* et ailleurs, avouant un plaisir volé, ces raisins par exemple sur le vignoble du propriétaire arabe, de ces rares bourgeois algériens d'El-Biar, qui nous menaça, Claude et moi, nous avions huit ou neuf ans, de nous remettre à la police après que son gardien nous eut pris la main sur la grappe, et ce fut l'éclat de rire nerveux quand il nous laissa partir en courant, depuis je suis les confessions de vol au cœur des autobiographies, la ventriloquie homosexuelle, la dette intraduisible, le ruban de Rousseau, les poires de sA, *nam id furatus sum, quod mihi abundabat et multo melius, nec ea re uolebam frui, quam furto appetebam, sed ipso furto et peccato. arbor erat pirus in uicinia nostrae uineae pomis onusta nec forma nec sapore inlecebrosis [...] non ad nostras epulas, sed uel proicienda porcis, etiamsi aliquid inde comedimus, dum tamen fieret a nobis quod eo liberet, quo non liceret. ecce cor meum, deus, ecce cor meum, quod miseratus es in imo abyssi,* comme si au-delà du besoin, mais encore ployé sur lui, le circoncis se caressait au vol de ce qu'il adresse à sa mère, te dis-je, ô mohel, en fouillant dans l'armoire de sa chambre, sous ses yeux qui ne me voient plus, chaque fois que je suis à Nice auprès d'elle pour constater qu'elle n'a presque rien gardé, quelques-unes, tout au plus, des cartes et lettres que je lui écrivis pendant près de trente ans, deux fois par semaine, sans parler des deux coups de téléphone dont le fantôme scande encore mes jeudis et dimanches matin, à l'heure où depuis douze mois j'ai cessé de l'appeler, elle ne répondra plus, ni bientôt à l'œil au bout des doigts aveugles, le 16, temps rauque, 93-84-13-32, ni tous ces numéros d'appel oubliés de ma vie.

ô fantôme de ma moleskine!

*L'adresse du Pardès où tout se décide pour Elie - Baba*

**47** 13, rue d'Aurelle-de-Paladines, El-Biar, c'est toujours le verger, le PaRDeS intact, le présent sans pli qui te continue, l'imperturbable phénomène que tu ne verras jamais vieillir, tu ne vieillis plus, bien qu'en ce jardin tout se décide, et la loi aussi loin que s'étende la mémoire, la mort de deux enfants, Jean-Pierre Derrida, le cousin, un an de plus que toi, écrasé par une automobile devant sa maison de Saint-Raphaël, à l'école on te dit ton frère est mort, tu le crois, un temps d'anéantissement dont tu n'es jamais ressuscité, et cinq ans plus tard, 1940, la mort de Norbert Pinhas, ton jeune frère cette fois, deux ans, puis l'expulsion du lycée comme de la francité, les jeux d'enfer avec Claude, Claude et Claudie, cousins cousines, tant de figues volées, à l'origine il y a le vol et le parjure, à la veille des 59 secrets d'Ali Baba, un indéchiffrable par jarre, à chaque date une goutte de sang, une date suffit à laisser le géologiciel sur place, comme celle que tu vis perler dans le dos de la petite fille qui se laisse distraitement enculer, à peine, avec des gestes sûrs mais aussi gauches que du mammifère à sa naissance, elle te sait bander sur le lit de ton père, tournée vers la radio, *numquid mentior aut mixtione misceo neque distinguo lucidas cognitiones harum rerum in firmamento caeli et opera corporalia*, cela signifie, suivez bien, que jamais tu n'écris comme sA, le père d'Adéodat dont la mère est sans nom, ni comme Spinoza, ils sont trop marranes, trop « catholiques », eût-on dit rue d'Aurelle-de-Paladines, trop loin du verger, ils disent le discours, comme le signe de circoncision, extérieur *ou* intérieur, non, non, tu as plus de deux langues, la figurale et l'autre, et il y a au moins 4 rabbins, au moins, « ... *"quant à leur longue existence comme* nation *dispersée ne formant plus un* État, *elle n'a rien de surprenant [...] et cela non seulement par l'observation des* rites extérieurs *opposés à ceux des autres nations, mais par* le signe de *la circoncision auquel ils restent religieusement attachés [...]. J'attribue une telle valeur en cette affaire au* signe de *la circoncision qu'à lui seul je le juge capable d'assurer à cette nation juive une existence éternelle. [...] De l'importance que peut avoir une particularité telle que la circoncision, nous trouvons un exemple remarquable chez les Chinois..."*, S. dit *"signe"* et *"rite extérieur"*, pourquoi ? *Revenir à l'original, plus tard, suite du texte, revoir : "signe de circoncision" et d'élection étranger à entendement et à vraie vertu »* (18-10-77), malgré ton désaccord avec lui sur ce point, et tu te rends toujours au-delà d'un désaccord, ose donc comparer la *schechina* de ton corps, celui du verger, à sa substance, et cela te réjouit, car tu penses alors à ce jeune homme, ancêtre du côté de ta mère, dont la cousine te dit qu'un jour, au matin du siècle dernier, il arriva du Portugal, je suis sûr que tu lui ressembles, tu ressembles de plus en plus à ta mère

ty through the magic of writing. A frenzy of activity. He'd like to believe in it, his substitute of a lie. He writes live right in the nick of time. There you have him, he who comes to life at the sound of a pun, who sniffs out and revives the verb *respire*, he mocks and swaps hats at the drop of a word— knowing we'll call him a liar just when he's telling the truth, for *respire* respirare, it really is re- or post-humous, come back from the dead; but then he never lies. Here's one liar who always never ceases to tell the truth and perfectly naturally, or at least so he writes. He writes as he posthumes. The writing is his survivor, she [*l'écriture, f.*] survives *him*.

I cannot emphasize enough that his whole philosophy is a consequence of the displacement of everyday language, a modern mocking of French as cliché. The writing surarrives and puts time out of joint, derails it, it makes its entry as the past-already while holding out the promise of the already-future that it is, that it will be. It makes your head spin, this whirligig of dates, pursued by anticipatory memory: I write in 1977 that which I shall rewrite in 1977–1989 and that will rewrite itself in 2077 as in 2002 as in 2088. The pen thinks and jests, an acrobat of a chirographer on the thread of time running out: it obeys the dictation of a violent and terribly fragile date, it makes its mark instantaneously past the pen knows it is ageless, O how lovely she is the one he calls "my survivress" he means *her*, my mother, my pen, my fellow voyager through the simulacra in which time's incredible verities masquerade. *List List O list* I am going to tell you the secret: there is no time, there are only dates, there is but one sea one mother forever surviving herself. And I when I "pass" from period 4 to period 42 I make believe *I pass*, for in fact I swim continuously from page to page among memories of the future and presentiments:

*"Recover the (lost) taste for holding the pen, for writing well which I have in a sense mistreated, retooled, long lost (double syntax of 'to lose someone') and, beyond the malediction which traverses my love for the person who has lost me,*

*rediscover an easy, offered, readable, relaxed writing"* (10–14–77), oh how fine your hands are, my survivress, she had such beautiful writing, that can be said in the past, quite different from mine, and very legible, graceful, elegant, more cultivated than she herself was, I wonder if that's possible, and how to speak of her and SA without participating in their chirography, from the tips of my toes to the ends of my fingers, without even feeling the resistance the substrate must have opposed to them both, but no more to you, G., nor to me, and I wonder again what can have happened when my writing changed, after thirty years

[after thirty years (of age? after a period of thirty years?)]

then again later, when machines took it over on the sea, for I got to the sea [ *gagné la mer*]

[some people reach land, shore; for him it's *la mer*—the sea—as if one could get to it without losing oneself, you must imagine a landing without land- ing, you must hear the sea singing the sea, calling it; not forgetting the *pied- noir* meaning of the word *gagner* (gain, reach, win), which on the other side of the sea meant to vanquish, overcome]

first against the current, against the waves from the screen that write on my face

[write = to be written by the sea, to be struck in the face, marked by the marine or maternal spittle that does not say its name or by these sobs]

to tell me how lucky my mother will be, if she is, to die before me, which I infer from my fear of not dying before my uncircumcised sons, objects of my infinite compassion, not that this compassion of mine be extended to all the uncircumcised but to my own, without religion apparently having anything to do with it, nor Moses the father of my mother, as for someone, me, who would be capable of inventing circumcision all by himself, as I do here.

[invent circumcision, there you have his dream and therefore his gesture. A de-Mosified circumcision, delivered from all genealogy, obedience, alliance. A circumcision unpolluted by legal paternity. Absolute. Absolved. Derridan. Neither gift nor debt. Neither memory nor inheritance. Nor religion. Look at it! He has just invented it, the ageless, faceless infant. He keeps it for himself, alone]

# VI

## POINT OF HONOR/POINT DONOR

### In which there is no mourning

The point to which the *point* is a thorn in his side, the whole corpus of his work bears the stigmata. The point is the absolute unity, without dimension, says mathematical discourse. The point is the true atom. The indivisible unity.

Now, the fundamental axiom of everything he says everywhere is the *divisibility of the point.*

Everything he writes, everything he thinks is a protest against the point as indivisible. He writes, divided, in order to divide it, the point. He thinks, he lives, divisibility, he divives [*divit*]. His sense of urgency on this point exceeds even his own calculations, sometimes he makes a point of attacking the point, sometimes it is his unconscious or the possibilities of the French language that work against the point. He does not admit the indivisible. This refusal is his point of honor. Never does he put a point, a dot, a period, the word, the sign, without a shudder. The one he is, whoever it may be, is never idle, never a fixed point. The minute he sights a point he is on his mark, he is off, he is gone. In the opposite direction. In all the opposite directions.

Everything he writes, he writes from the starting point aiming always for the point that is furthest beyond. I could cite thousands of examples. Here's one chosen at random: *Un Ver à Soie*, begins on an airplane with this sentence

> **Before the Verdict, mine,** before the sentence falls and drags me down with it, before it is too late, stop writing. *No point in writing [ne point écrire].*
>
> (*Veils*, P. 25; MY EMPHASIS)

It's him in a nutshell this vertiginous manner of expressing something, to begin by *writing no point in writing*, to play, to outplay the point, to wish in writing not to write any more, to dream therefore of not writing the point (period), on the one hand not to write—this is a dream—on the other to write without a period (point), without end, enjoin (oneself) to write pointlessly before it is too late, what an idea! It is thus necessary not to write anything before the fall, to write only too late, no point (period) except in the fall? No point (period) in writing in sum. No point (period) in writing *here* in the space-time before the end. Write then only in the end.

He doesn't say not to write you will note, he points to the point, he makes his point by point. Pointedly. He didn't say not to write [*ne pas écrire*]. *Pas* means *step* and has to do with walking. The *point* has to do with space.

On purpose? I have no idea. The sentence always comes along on its own.

In the case in point, it will have come along, twisted with apprehension, bowed by the wind of imminence. Imminence of what? It is always death that immines, one doesn't even need to name it, one must not. When there is imminence one can only be on the point, the point of. To keep to the point, an awkward position, and tease it out in submultiples. One ought to give meticulous thought to the expression that recurs in *Le Ver à Soie, on the point of.* To think about the quasi-infinite multiplication of the point, before it becomes the final point. To live the Before is the project of *Le Ver à Soie.* Knit by *casting off stitch-*

*es* he says. In this way one weaves toward the final stitch, or the last word: the smaller than any finite quantity and yet this point is not nothing. There are millions of instants in the last moment, if you can slow it down enough. On the point. Itching to be gone. Soon gone. All too soon. In the meantime—one sees that the feverish factorizaton of the point in *Le Ver à Soie* has always aimed at survival, the ruse of life in order to give the end the slip.

Before death there is lots of time, just before death there is still time. An infinitesimal space but a space nonetheless. He has always practiced this saving deproximation. Between the Jew and him the Jew they tell him he is, between what, without qualms and without consideration, one is accustomed to term Jewish he has always insisted on introducing the tip [*la pointe*] of a precaution in order to fend off the verdict's fatality the truth-saying of the verdict, this sense of being condemned and executed that is ineluctably engendered by the incredible circumcision scene. Circumcised without his consent, before any word, before passivity even.

The point, the identifiable, the undeniable, the whole of his philosophy contests it.

The minute he risks capture, he begins to struggle. He will never agree to be taken either for a Jewish Jew, or as a photo, at least not without putting up a fight. Even if he forces himself to consent. Look what happened with the filming of *D'ailleurs Derrida*, as it is described in *Tourner les mots*, on the one hand with implacable humor by the Author Safaa Fathi, on the other hand with implacable humor by himself in the role of Actor.

A circus of concessions extracted under duress. They argue. About this or that. Apparently. As soon as it begins it starts up again

with these words:

Thus, lowering my guard even before making up my mind, even before turning around, I allow myself be taken by surprise.

Even today I don't know why or by whom.

The filming had already begun.

Never had I consented to this point. And yet never had the consenting been so anxious about itself, so little and so poorly played, painfully devoid of complacency.

(Tourner les mots, P. 73)

The word <i>circumcision</i> has not been pronounced. In its place: <i>point</i>. Never did I consent to this point he says. A tone of protest? Or denial?

But the thread, the filament, of the film and the ancient filiations have never been cut.

Had she not been Egyptian and a woman if she hadn't been Egypt and he in this case the figure of the Algerian Jew, if the blind memories of these countries had not been secretly at work, would he have consented to this point? I mean to <i>this</i> point? <i>Punctum caecum</i> he had said in neutral Latin. A neutral point. A blind point. To this point, says the other, I would not have consented ever.

# VII

## CIRCUMFICTIONS OF A CIRCUMCISION OBJECTOR

It is all said to have begun behind his back without his consent without his seeing it. If only, before all seeing, all looking, he could have seen the blow coming.

Circumcision, how to be there? At one's own? Now there is a primal scene, doubtless the only one at which the main character will not have been present. Not been invited. For his own he was not there, not by choice, he was there without being there, a hostage of the heritage. It happened to him while he was still a little absent barely present and he was struck by it. And it is this incredible, impossible event that makes him a person born condemned, born robbed, the blind man the injured party, as one says in French of the one who has not received his birthright, his legacy, and therefore suffers, as a result of this confiscation, this lack, an unhealable wound. Whence this transformation of injured party into zealous person in other words into jealous person, jealous with an endless jealousy, jealous of himself the other that he was going to be and was not, jealous of what escapes him at the very instant of the debt falling due. Magnificent he describes this jealousy of the circumcised Jew to himself, jealous I confess to being and I must say there is cause to be furious, I understand him like my brother, blind jealousy always already/ousy [*déjalousie*], jealousy of the blind, he who does not see himself being seen, the frightful torment, I can feel it with my eyes, of one who feels himself the passive or impotent object of what gazes, that was the suffering of Samson, *eyeless in Gaza*, from the wound flows the blood and images of me that go about the streets and I am helpless to stop them . My enemies laugh at me and I do not see them laugh.

Blind circumcision—(for) it sees not what it does, all its executors are deprived of the scope of their action by millennia of obedience—a child whose sight is not yet hatched—but at eight days he can see thirty centimeters, the knife, does he see it? *und war/schon nicht/entaügt*, being not yet reft of eyes as Celan says ("Mandelnde" in *Zeitgehöft*). And the lyre? A day of absolute passivity, which cannot occur save at the expense of the most powerful repression. Day of faith and unreason. Day of amputation. Amputation, what a word! Day of pruning back thought, of purification *as* thought, day of *thought-putatio*-all-around, day of turning around what turns around circumcision. *Amputatio* day of thought cut and cutting. Day of judgment and of execution. Circumcision is the first case of a verdict. Later and forever afterward he will be interested in circumcision, he is the outcome of this operation, and, let us note, interested by choice or perforce, for he says *"that's what interests me and tells me not how I am a case but wherein I am no longer a case"* (period 14).

I pause a moment—Klein silences his stick in front of Gross because here I am sticking my neck out me a woman me the uncircumcised, a least in appearance, speaking of the fate that is not our lot. Lot of the man. Sexual discrimination. Suffering, crime, memory, trace—reserved. For men circumcision for women, I emphasize, noncircumcision, or perhaps circumcision-by-alliance.

Therefore I cannot discuss circumcision, I cannot not discuss it, with all due circumcispection, I can talk about it from the sidelines as sister and daughter of sometimes-circumcised sometimes-not Jews and right away there's the question, up it pops with its scissors ready to separate the foreskin from the glans, Jewish-Jew from Non-Jewish-Jew, circumcised-Jew from non-circumcised Jew all the same or maybe not, it all depends on the question, where you draw the line that sorts them out, yes, the minute I want to start talking about circumcision I find myself cut off, barred, stopped, tortured with questions, racked with indecision mine and that of my sons father brother, all of us who turn very diversely and each in turn to each his torments around this blow in the dark this most ancient of oft-told tales, this operation, this action, this catastrophe, this thing of the body which is of the mind, this incarnation of the capital Verb on the member of a small one, this mythical invention whose tenacity rivals with genetic transmission, this violence, says my son, "the supposed crime that I call circumcision" he says, the crime par excellence.

The infant's cry sounds just like one of ours being baptized Montaigne muses anthropological witness of a Judeo-Roman circumcision (*Journal de voyage en Italie*).

The child, then, cries, cries Jewish as Christian, cries Judeo-Christian, cries no more no less. It is a point of hearing.

Here is the scene, viewed from Rome. Rome as Paris as Algiers. Montaigne dates it: January 30, 1581. He gives us all the details. We see that he has eyes only for the mohel. As for the child, it cries like any child. A quarter of an hour is all it takes.

On the table at which this godfather is seated, there is a great preparation of all the instruments that are needed for this operation. In addition to that, a man holds a phial full of wine and a glass in his hands. There is also a brazier on the ground, over which this man first warms his hands, and then, finding the child's clothes undone, as the godfather holds it on his lap with its head towards him, he takes hold of its member and pulls the skin which covers it back towards him, with one hand, while with the other he pushes the glans and the member within. Over this skin which he holds towards the said glans, he lays a silver instrument which maintains the skin in place, and prevents him, cutting it, from injuring the glans and the flesh. After that, with a knife, he cuts off this skin, which they promptly bury in a pan of earth which is there with the rest of the preparations for this mystery. After that, with his bare nails, the minister wrinkles up some other pellicule of skin which is on this glans and rips it off, and pushes it back behind the glans. It seems that there is a great deal of effort in this and pain;

On January 31 he [Montaigne] had an attack of colic and passed a biggish stone. At this moment (of the story) our Jacques Derrida feels violent sympathy in the region of his lower belly.

As soon as this glans is thus bared, they make haste to give some wine to the minister who puts a little in his mouth, and goes off thus to suck the glans of this child, all bloody, and spits out the blood that he has drawn from it, and forthwith takes as much wine again, up to three times. That done they give him a twist of paper with some red powder they say is dragon's blood, with which he sprinkles and covers the wound; and then wraps the member of this child up very cleanly in bandages cut to size for this purpose. That done, they give him a full glass of wine, which wine they say he blesses by saying some prayers over it. He takes a swig of it, then dipping his finger into it he thrice gives the child a few drops to suck on the tip of his finger; and afterwards they send this glass, in this same state, to the mother and to the women who are in some other part of the house, to drink what remains of the wine.

How to turn around a wound, he wonders if it is "mine"—how to do this, how to turn around my mouth, my lips, my sex, what a question, and around *my* wound that is even more terrifying, can I say *my* wound of this opening by which the stranger's part is incised in me? But if *I* can not turn around *me*, an I can turn around the words. He saves the words, the syllables, of the cunning question, he turns around *turn, around, wound, as, if.* With all the remains marks signs scars he makes his sparks. Economy, economy. *Thrift, thrift. Spare. Scar.* To be sparing. The savings, the sparing of what will not have spared him, the *escarre*—the one he calls my jealousy. The *escarre* he exchanges and that exchanges him with Esther.

❖ ❖ ❖ ❖ ❖ ❖ ❖ ❖ ❖ ❖

You hear him *growing a new skin*, first he makes it, he puts himself to death next he stitches himself up again, he rises, living, there he is remade, everything is to be recontinued

so long as I have not written a treatise *marking* the origin and end of my jealousy, *Of the indubitable foundation or the* cogito *of my jealousy*, or again *The Confessions of a Mother*, I will have wasted my life and written nothing

. . .

I am overfond of words because I have no language of my own, only false *escarres*, false foci (*eskhara*), those blackish and purulent scabs that form around the wounds on my mother's body

*Escarre* oh cruel *caress* gone mad.

It is to Circumcision, his *significance*, his solemn engagement [*sa fiance*] signed in his absence, that he owes planetary verbal circulation and this dechronization, this circumcision of the ends of the cord of time that runs through him, for if time is circular and its ends merge, then it is here at the end of before and after that a revolutionary psychology is born to him, such that he will be *preceded* by his sentiments, always preceded, just imagine, preceded and preferred, preceded preferred perdu lost. Here play on all the possibilities of the expression: *ils m'ont perdu*, they lost me: they no longer have me; they brought about my downfall. Lost for them lost for him saved for him. Lost save. Circumcision was his loss, was the loss of him. From which come all these divisions, these splits [*écarts*], these *ec*, these arts, these *rac*, all this straddling of the self, I draw (myself) apart [*je m'écarte*] he says, I quarter myself [*je m'écartèle*], I stand apart from her [*je m'écarte d'elle*], *je m'ec-* as Genet would say, I am in pieces, I cut myself, oh! I am cut as one guilty of self-betrayal would say *inadvertently* for he never betrays himself, only betrayal betrays him/I have cut myself, I have cut the tip of my finger myself, I quarter myself, cut after cut I cannot avoid

all these splits vying beneath the trembling silk of the self which must nonetheless say *I*

all these divisions at work within him causing him the continuous and fruitful suffering of the soul's dislocation.

Dislocated, delocalized, dislodged, disconcerted by the expression "in my place" [*chez moi*] is what he is, promptly separated from himself, interrupted, but not by himself, he is seven or eight days old, that's it, he loses his head, that of his member, there is blood, the scene once described in detail by Montaigne is each time the same scene, that of January 30, 1581, mankind's most ancient religious ceremony: the cirumcision of the Jews. Rite of alliance and of exclusion of the entry and the exit, separation of the penis, separation of the self and subsequently separation of the world henceforth into two worlds, on the one hand the *in,* the within, the among, the like, the in-common, on the other hand, the *out,* the other, the not like. And so on to the end of the ends of the time of times.

True it is the lot of all human beings, to be born, come out, be severed weaned.

But for the Jew, the male child, the passage from the maternal enclosure to the outside air, the border crossing, the expulsion delivery—

is repeated, and within eight days, blow by blow. Along comes circumcision to put its visible and legible stamp on the barely published little body. Not without a great deal of effort and pain. Nowadays circumcision takes place under anesthesia in a hospital setting. Thus one imagines one does away with the violence. Another takes its place.

The next day Montaigne had a touch of colic and passed some stones. This is a *Jewish story*, it is even the story of the Jews, their first new beginning—every "so-called Jew" knows it so well he no longer knows it, most of them never give it a thought what's done is done that's how it is and always will be, for my brother it's a trifle, my brother the circumcised father of uncircumcised sons like Derrida, I mean like Derrida circumcised father of the uncircumcised.

For my mother the German always prepared to grant rituals their letters patent of reason, it's healthy, it's hygienic, Jews she says—and perhaps believes—have always been at the forefront of progress, says my mother the German from Osnabrück who does not believe in God, all of them, in this half deported half disseminated family don't believe in God, but say the word Jew, I am Jewish, they believe themselves Jewish that doesn't stop you considering yourself Jewish, but for my brother the hygiene business is a joke, it's a social gesture he says.

If Elie is present at each circumcision, at the birth of each male child, then the question is present, to circumcise or not, you have to make up your mind.

Circumcision turns around the family, like a crow with scissor wings, sometimes it alights, sometimes it doesn't, but it never misses a cradle, it flies in circles around the infant's Moses basket. Elie is going to feed the crow.

It's always about the *né*—the newborn, the nose—in the Bible as in religion, what the sacrifice theme wants is the *né*. The newborn male, son of a Jewish woman you've heard of her, that paradox, that missing link: the Jewish wife has no place in the Jewish circle, and yet there can be no true circumcision if the excluded mother is not known to be the daughter of a Jewish woman. She is not Jewish, she has no bar mitzvah and no tallith, she is not among the Jews in the synagogue, she is off to the side, she is apart, she is parked in the balcony, she is there to look at him—her son her brother her spouse her lover her father, she is the overlooked essential, the witness excluded for millennia who is nonetheless bizarrely necessary, from far away and right under your nose.

But those women daughters of Jewish women talk, without the right, nothing but duties. Many of them, most of the ones I've known in any case feel they are what they are not, Jewish that is, out of love out of fidelity. They are uncircumcised, therefore circumcised.

So what do they do? They make the best of a bad thing. They cook, the cooking is primordial. In the old days, the women of G. née Safar's generation would play cards. That too is vital. You have to consider these activities for the metaphors they are.

It's all metaphor. Circumcision as well. Forbidden and unthinkable and unthought of for women, female circumcision did exist, in hiding, in secret. I can hear them, Georgette, Esther, Omi my grandmother, my Aunt Erika, each in her own language, saying: I cut! I call my mother to make sure of this: how does one say "I cut" in German? *Ich schneide* says my mother, whereupon she cuts me off. They cut therefore and they are cut. Everything is fiction and everything is reality. Circumcision is all around us and we don't know it.

It's always the *né* as you know. Or the *nez* [nose] in French. My too-long too-big nose my oversize appendage and childhood fear. Chop it off, says my mother. I was fourteen at the time. And I almost did. True this is a scene with two meanings, a double circle moving in opposite directions. I was about to have my nose trimmed, I didn't do it. I was afraid of running away from my signifier, my né-Jewish too big too long nose, my tip of an organ my father. In this way I had myself circumcised in reverse by refusing the operation. There are more kinds of circumcision than we think.

So with or without God how does one become Jewish? If not first of all by Jewsay.

To me says my mother Eve Klein, it means belonging to an ethical group that has always been persecuted that helped each other out. They were family men hard workers. We won't talk about the others. You got married, that was an obligation. In Algiers there was a rabbi who was queer it was quite a problem because it's strictly forbidden for Jews to have relations in that way. I've heard of it but it's not something you talk about. Says my mother. In any case he was supposed to marry young. For the Sephardim at least.

Now the Ashkenazi speaks: I also remember Tirza Feuchtwanger, the family of Gemen who is English now, with her ten children she had twins and for one they didn't know if it was a boy or a girl. So the father Otto the rabbi said what a nuisance it's strictly forbidden for Jews to be abnormal.

Being a Jewish woman? I asked—Those two cousins who can't get married because they are neither orthodox nor secular, neither one thing or the other. Says my mother. Our generation doesn't exist any more, when you were Jewish with or without God, with or without faith, simple beings with a nice mellow Judaism worn but not threadbare nonviolent roomy, accommodating, German. That lot have totally vanished. Now either they're black or they don't exist. Says my mother. Black? I say. The beards, says my mother. So many different kinds and species.

In the family we're all true false Jews. It's true we're not really Jewish but it doesn't suffice to say it. It suffices to say it for it to become false. If you don't say it, it becomes false as well. One can't however not. We say we're Jewish so as not to say the contrary. But we don't say we are not so as not to offend the religion that we respect and don't have. We have an idea of the thing we've never had.

—Montaigne used to say the Jews are among the oldest people in religion I say.

—That's what I meant says my mother, we're the most ancient in religion. But in 1934 already I had the most modern apartment.

Besides I'd say *ich bin Jüdisch*. I wouldn't say *ich bin eine Jüdin*, remarks my mother. Some people used to say *Israeliten, keine Juden*, it was less offensive they thought she says.

Circumcision of circumcision, he says. Some people circumcise circumcision by saying *Communion* instead of Bar Mitzvah. Others say *Israelite*, the politer, more genteel term, so as not to say Jews. It's all fiction. It's all circumfiction.

Not to circumcise is also a decision, a cision cut from circum, a circumcised cision, it leaves a scar. He himself relates to his uncircumcised sons from his circumcision to their noncircumcision. It puts a little distance between them in which to raise the question: why circumcision? Has he decircumcised himself or undecircumcised himself in the noncircumcision of his sons, uncircumcised that is circumcised in reverse, cut off from circumcision by some parental decision in which the son had no part, as before him the father child, some kind of decision taken by the parents or by the unconscious? Was there, and if so why, an attempt at Eli-mination or at auto-Eli-mination or at resistance to Eli-mitation?

"Why-circumcision?" remains, question, always to be done and therefore as if never yet done, and still, done once in the past, it goes on repeating itself, it begins again, one can not stop oneself, try as one occasionally will to turn it around, to leave in the opposite direction, one finds oneself back nose to nose with it, it's the old ring trick, the god has got the man in a lasso.

There are even those who go so far as to conceal it, their circumcision or their noncircumcision, as if it were possible. Only he, the philosopher of philosophers, has paced out the millenary archives of this most living aporia: renewed, alliance or no alliance, at the birth of every so-called Jewish boy. First he bled, then he signed. This is the origin of his work of art, of his works: his sons, circumcised figuratively for not having been so in their flesh.

And this is how he can state, "I am the last of the Jews," without boasting one could hardly better disrepudiate the fiction that contains the truth. Only the defiancéd Jew who speaks French and bears in French the name of Derrida can one day have made such a strategicomic profession of faith. After the last of the Jews what or who can one be waiting for, what follow up, succession, coming or extinction? What ashes or phoenix? Unless it was necessary *to hear* the phrase outplay itself at the moment of its utterance? Perhaps he meant to say I am *the last de-Jew*? He who announces a generation of re-Jews? Don't let's forget he is capable of anything. Nothing of what he seems to say will ever be able to be used against him.

Circumcision-fiction.

To which circumcision and fiction he is attached. What upsets him is to be held to it, or that it hold him, as if there had been a rape, rape by alliance or for alliance, as is always the case one must concede when the scene takes place between the too big Allpowerful and the little guy, prophet or not, who does His Will—he is attached, tenuously, to Circumcision but he stipu-lates—wherever he talks about it, *to Circumcision as a figure.*

> I am not even able to say that this so improbable figure of "turning around" a wound can translate for me an experience of or an approach to Judaism. The question remains to know what Judaism is as a figure, pre-cisely; and what circumcision is as a figure. And fundamentally, in what-ever manner I interpret or one interprets the fact that, they tell me, I was born a Jew or am circumcised, I always come back to, or I always find myself up against a problem of figure, a *"cas de figure"* as they say in French.
>
> (*Questions au judaïsme*, P. 75)

The question remains. It remains forever in the vicinity of Judaism or of the *circumfigure*.

"I always find *myself* [*myself* is emphasized] up against a problem of figure, a case in point, a *'cas de figure'* as they say in French." He turns in the neighborhood, he would like to get away and everything brings him back *before* a problem of figure. The sentence itself, which is performative, poses a "a problem of figure," a figurative and semantically ambiguous expression in French. The myself [*me*] is French too, it is this ambiguous *me*, it looks reflexive but not exactly. When he finds himself it is always before a *cas de figure*, a case in point. One might say: facing it. Face to face with himself, he doesn't find himself except figuratively. But not only. Once again, behind the word *figure* one hears the rhetorical term, *figure, trope, tropos, turn,* the figure by which a word or expression is diverted from its rightful destination, abducted.

He only finds *himself* before, in front of, a case of abduction, before the event, some figurative accident, collision, damage facial paralysis for example or his immobilization faced with the enigma of the question: Am I Jewish, they tell me I am, what is Jewish, etc. So the question remains to be faced, to be figured out:

AM I JEWISH OR DO I FLEE FROM JEWISH? [*SUIS-JE JUIF OU FUIS-JE JUIF?*]

*Fuis-je juif?* This paragram can torment the subject only in French. But who, among those whose ears were grazed by this word, the word *Jew,* in their childhood, has not shuddered at the furtive step this paragram takes? Especially if their childhood, like Jacques Derrida's, was surrounded by the echoes of war?

I heard this sentence rustling at the window. It was not alone. Sister sentences from other anguished consciences came to join it. Like the one that suddenly cracks open Rousseau's *Confessions,* so powerful it leaves a scar, a trace, and therefore wellspring for the sentences that followed upon it. Here it is, forever trembling:

"Was I happy? No, I had a taste of pleasure" (*Confessions,* book 5).

Every great book contains a sentence that signs it in secret blood. That one, that infinitely crazed sentence, is the secret of Rousseau's *Confessions*: it is the question he can't shake off. It is still there vibrating not long before his death. It is his arrow. The arrow of wounded and wounding happiness. He was *made* happy without having asked for it: what a misfortune. One *must not* be happy. The sharpness of it is so precise that it pierces the flesh of books and turns up later in the side of Proust. "I ought to have been happy: I wasn't," says the child struck with happiness. All these sons stricken with adoring mothers, pierced by a cruel turn of the gift, weaned without warning by one superfluous caress, doomed to be pursued by this subversion of happiness: "Was I," they wonder, was I am I, shall I have been, "timorous, courageous, a good writer" (Stendhal). No. But. "I had a taste of pleasure." To each his question. But the response is always the same. *Was I Jewish? now I wonder* wonders Jacques Derrida. *No, I had a taste of pleasure.* What sort of pleasure? The pleasure of not. The pleasure called no. The pleasure *for*, in place of being happy, Jewish, timorous, joyous, genial, orphaned. That's what the taste of pleasure is: a taste of not-being, which is a bitter form of the taste of being. The pleasure of not-to-be, which opens to the series of replacements of me by a whole pack of others. *Was I Jewish or do I flee being Jewish?* He asks himself, the question, the figure of ever further, *from the very first page* of the notebooks, and he says *I'm dating this* once again playing both the date and the circumcision that had already occurred in *Schibboleth* as in his flesh. Because it does not stop will never stop happening to him as date, as dated, as *data*, as *Ursache* of his speech.

❖  ❖  ❖  ❖  ❖  ❖  ❖  ❖  ❖  ❖

Did you hear him? It's all he can talk about. *Ça* or circumcision. How's that written, *ça* or *sa*? Or *SA*? Who knows? And the gender as well, we aren't to know whether it is neuter or masculine or if it tends toward or has a penchant for the feminine; if *ça* is the demonstrative pronoun, or if it's *ça* the adverb of place; or that so very French interjection without which we would be at a loss to express our stupefaction. In any case all that [*tout ça*] always evokes the Freudian *Ça* (id), the genial name for the unconscious commander.

His entire philosophy, he suspects, will perhaps have been a rehashing of the innumerable figures of the Circumcision figure, or perhaps it speaks only of that in an incessant kaleidoscope of changes or maybe it is itself but one link in the chain of substitutions, one can always dash around the ring or the circle in order to try and find the inexistent door.

But all the same, that relay race came to a halt, *once*, the one and only day—there is still always the unique instant in the great wheel of time—and that was July 23, 1930, the day of the scene that for him defies all accounts of it.

*Circumcision,* in any case, is a word he's attached to, less to the word *Jew,* perhaps hardly at all, poor Jew word they showed him it's like the word *Jüdisch*, and even the word *Jewish*, in the end during the war my mother would say of another he's a J.

But the circumcision word, in French, is inexhaustible, it's too good to go without now that he's salvaged it from the cultural shipwreck he is attached to its *si* as to its *comme* as to its *con* as to the apple of his eye he holds to his *mes (sie) circoncision*.

*"always attach the greatest importance, in anamnesis, to the fact that in my fam-*
*ily and among the Algerian Jews, one almost never said 'circumcision' but 'bap-*
*tism,' not Bar Mitzvah but 'communion,' with the consequence of the softening,*
*dulling, through fearful acculturation, from which I have always suffered more*
*or less consciously, of unavowable events, felt as such, not 'Catholic,' violent, bar-*
*barous, harsh, 'Arab,' circumcision, circumcised, interiorised, secretly assumed*
*accusation of ritual murder" (20–12–76)* . . .

whereas in my home, in my unbelieving family that had brought a minimum of cultural baggage along with it from Germany, if the Sephardic half lay dozing in amnesia, the unamnesiac Ashkenazi half could read the Bible in Hebrew—that was the female half, note—and never would we have said baptism or communion nary a Catholic uncatholic word in the house.

And the father? His father, Aimé, that's his name from the Hebrew Haim he says (Haim which only means Life in Hebrew, that is, everything though not necessarily the person loved [*l'être aimé*]), I find him off to one side, in the corner of the Circumcision painting, discreet, yet it is he who gives the name according to the law, all the names. He is a reserved sort of man. It's not with him Jacques Derrida plays his games. The initiation is her doing. But poring over the texts and with time I see him loom larger, he comes into focus in *La Contre-Allée*. He is back at the wheel and one discovers what he bequeathed to his son: the Derridan Voyage, a Voyaging compulsively ordered by the other, as if he had, Jacques Derrrida, always unconsciously obeyed the paternal paving of the way.

The Voyage, deconstructed, off the tracks, Odyssean, contrary-minded, the Voyage out in order to come back, that's him, the father he calls *my poor father*, poor scapegoat of a traveler emissary of the Catholic firm Tachet, he says "the expiatory victim," subject of his compassion. A portrait all the more poignant for its brevity. From him he gets that work does not serve to earn a living but to pay for disappearance. Was Aimé ever brought out of bondage?

For the son, the poor father will not have been a wine salesman in vain. There is a kind of vengeance affect, of vindicating the father, that blows through (blasts) the work of the son. As if he had also wished to redeem, gently convert the humiliating "rounds" of Aimé, the beloved traveler, into *tours*. Gloriously good-for-nothing on the mother's side voyaged by the father beyond any voyages hitherto known to us, it is perhaps in order to love Aimé, or in his memory that Jacques Derrida lets something utterly new come to light in his thought these days: what lies beyond the death wish. The dead are not as dead as we believe. The father comes back. Each time the son recalls him(self).

*Circumcision returns*, although it only happens once—(but) in appearance it recommences. One time [*une foi-s*], he insists. Circumcision insists.

What does *une fois* mean in French *une fois*, when it is *said in French* carries faith [*la foi*] along with it in homonymy, and every time he says *une foi* it is the other time [*l'autre fois*], faith/time turns on itself, indeed that is what it means, turn, *vicem*, *vez*, he likes to spin *une fois* vertiginously. And the expression that haunts him, that keeps coming back in all his texts now, like the leitmotiv of his desire to be done with it, is *une fois pour toutes*—once and for all—to be done with the finite. With the *finiteJew* he is among others or as one would say in French *le fieffé Juif*, the arrant fief of a Jew—that is, the de-enfeoffed, or as he says, mockingly, with the last of the Jews.

Circumcision comes back, the umpteenth circumcision. There is the one he describes in *Schibboleth* as "one single time, circumcision . . .

1. *One single time: circumcision occurs but once.*

2. At least such is *the appearance we are given* . . .

3. *We must turn around* this appearance.

The one that sets the tropic of circumcision in motion, the Derridan meridian, still the same and always the first.

And then there is the one that took place but once, and in reality, Jackie's. His circumcision before any possibility of faith. That of July 23, 1930, which was also his mother's birthday. That circumcision is not an example, nor a figure. Thus from the first he is circumcised at least twice, to be brief circumcised literally and figuratively, in his flesh and forever, and circumcised like all poets, like all men circumcised by language or with an inclination to circumcise language.

All men are therefore circumcised. Let's translate he says lest we forget, by the same trope therefore all women also . . . Thus we are all translated and in translation—circumcised. He has always known, prudence and respect, not to take anything for himself not even, especially not the disappropriation that accompanies Jews as Celan puts it. Disappropriated and circumcised like you and me. He's not the sort to fall into the trap of the paradoxical overbidding of identification by nonidentity to oneself:

> insofar as the Jew's identity to himself or to Judaism *would* consist in this exemplariness, that is in a certain non-identity with oneself, "I am this" meaning I am this and universal," well, the more one dislocates one's self-identity, the more one says "my own identity consists in not being identical to myself, in being a foreigner, the non-coinciding with the self," etc. the more Jewish one is! And at that point, the word, the attribute "Jewish," the quality of "Jewish" or of "Judaism" are locked in a spiral of overbidding. It allows one to say that the less one is what one is, the more Jewish one is, and, consequently, the less one is Jewish, the more Jewish one is. . . . The logical proposition "I am Jewish" thus loses any kind of assurance, it gets carried away in ambition, a kind of pretension, a spiral of overbidding!
>
> (*Questions au judaïsme*)

So not a JewishJew not Jew-itself not more or less Jewish but Jewish-like-Celan-who-was-Jewish-like-Marina-Tsvetayeva-who-was-Jewish-as-poet-who-was-Jewish like all those who are born in order not to inhabit the hyper-Christian city she says in *Poem of the End* (1924), born to be expulsed, born to have no other roof than the thou-roof [*toi/toit*] of language, born into language, and born *of* language, born to the language which goes before us and commands us, whose secrets we will later worm out, Jewish like Ancel turned inside-out to make the poet Celan himself the poet torn tearing the German language to shreds, the syllable dancer, Celan the brilliant word-breaker, and Jewish like his sister in letters Tsvetayeva under whose aegis Celan writes, and to whom he dedicates the most poem of poems, the poem

"Und von dem Buch aus Tarussa." On several occasions, Derrida recalls the epigraph of this poem (from *Die Niemandsrose*), so that, at the end of its race out of Russian it ends up in French translation in these words: "Tous les poètes sont des Juifs (All poets are Jews)." Only three words here where a book would scarcely suffice to tell of the encounter and the *conversation-conversion* of Tsvetayeva-Celan-Derrida into one another.

1. First to note Tsvetayeva's passion-revolution, the manner in which she *affirms* her *elective Judaism*, her Judaism as figure of the poet-being. Oh the beauty of this embracing of the people that proclaims itself elect, therefore not electing.

2. To give briefly the original version of Tsvetayeva's exclamation, as quoted moreover by Celan *in Russian* (and that, in my view, ought to have remained in Russian when it was translated into French): *Poety-zhidy*: Poets— Yids! Yids *Zhidi* but consonant with *zhizn,* life. As in *Jewlive*. These words, shouted out, form the last line of a broken, chopped up, en-raged monologue (in *Poem of the End*) that in six strophes works out the theme of banishment as common to poets and Jews, in a dazzling, performative dislocation of the idiom. And among the words subjected to her blade or knife, I mean to Tsvetayeva's steely pen, is the other word, the more genteel way of saying Jew in Russian: *Ev-rejski* (Heb-rew), which she cuts. And see what happens when this word *Evreiski* is circumcised: it is then heard as, read as Eve—separated united from Rei, paradise.

3. To point out the necessity of Celan's poem, which commemorates and reawakens interest in the other, in the other poet Tsvetayeva but also therefore in poets as Jews, as the ex-pulsed, as the exiled, as pilgrims of the pen, wanderers, speakers of words and singers of sounds with neither shelter nor monument. An immense poem, set in motion, re/jected by its first line, composed of the single vocable *Vom*. Vom, a contraction of *von dem*, the preposition that speaks of *ex*pulsion, of distancing at the same time as belonging, the origin as point of departure, copula of the genitive objective and subjective,

translated into French as *de* (of, from): beating afterward throughout with the German word *von*, which tells of the origin, the departure, the detachment, the way-making, the going-awayness. *The going-awayness alliance.*

Who am I, *me*? Who will reply to the question he keeps asking Georgette Sultana Esther Mummy if you like, in order to make her avow, her in me, me outside her, outside myself and wild about it? What kind of a Jew am I or do I flee from being? In the end he will have thought of and evoked it all without ever composing a *sum*, there is no *ergo*, no conclusion to wrap it up, round and round he goes, extenuated, on the nostalgia carousel, harnessing this who-am-I which inevitably turns up on the tongue, in the language, to one or another attribute or epithet that makes our heads spin in French: I am the end of Judaism, last of the Jews that I am, advancing in a cloud of eschatalogical dust, having renounced and yet still searching, in the vague space of a nonannullable errancy, for a kind of response in replacement, an origin, an impossible beginning now in tragic mode, now in comic, one false step and one plummets into the other register; being the last of the Jews is comic after all, that's his ruffian side, or on the other hand parodying God, with a whole theory of I ams, for example: I am the Order. Look for him in *La Carte Postale* (p. 272), "The Epistles there's my novel" the author states. And then enumerates himself: first Paul (the little brother dead before me) next Jacques therefore next Pierre and Jean.

I am not myself therefore, not Jewish-self at least so far as I know, or feel or live, Jewish if you insist, a Jew as if, but *concesso non dato* eh—*circoncesso*—I merely concede, for the time being. As Kafka circumceded, *"Man kann doch nicht nicht juden"*—Yet one cannot not Jew [*juivre*].

In the end he is so fed up with this saw, I am tired, tired sick of it [*marre*]. And that's when the figure of the Marrano comes to him—like an unheralded messiah—not so long ago—perhaps ten or twelve years ago. Coming from a book—coming as a present from a son—the Marrano is the coming, his coming—right away he takes to it. Lost, he finds himself again in this figure, it's him without a doubt, that's me, face to face with myself suddenly. Unfindable, even in dictionaries.

When he declared himself the last of the Jews, he didn't know how apt it was, the last of the last, and after, the worst and most precious. The last talks to himself. Who else remains to remind of your presence? So it was the Marrano he was calling, the Marrano that he already was although he didn't know it. One of those Jews without knowing it and without knowledge, Jew without having it, without being it, a Jew whose ancestors are gone, cut off, as little Jewish as possible, the disinheritor, guardian of the book he doesn't know how to read, half buried and all the more tenacious for that. He who dreams of tunneling under the ground of the circle, of the house of the circular temple and escaping, or who'd dream of being lifted up from the host and hostage scene as Elijah was removed from the persecution of the faithful Elisha, from above, all in flames, he who would like to escape the cruel circus of inheritance, he's tired of inheriting and leaving legacies. But it was only a dream.

And suddenly here's someone who got away, he surges up blinking his eyes, it's a mole—the blessed disinheriting it's him, the remainder guardian of what remains. The Celant, the self-concealed, still a little maroon, fugitive I mean.

Here's one who, if there's such a thing as faith, has got it. He prays and does not know what he says.

To think he was a Marrano all along and didn't know it. A true Marrano. Don't tell a soul. It's a secret. He confided it to himself in Toledo in these terms:

> it's that if I am a sort of *Marrano* of French Catholic culture, and I also have my Christian body, inherited from SA in a more or less twisted line, *condiebar eius sale*, I am one of those *Marranos* who no longer say they are Jews even in the secret of their own hearts, not so as to be authenticat-

ed *Marranos* on both sides of the public frontier, but because they doubt everything, never go to confession or give up enlightenment, whatever the cost, ready to have themselves burned, almost.

(PERIOD 33)

Marrano, the sublime figure of Oblivion in which memory keeps watch, dozes off, more Marrano than ever, about the wide earth he goes, running away. From himself. He attends to safeguarding the unknown, the stranger he is.

Alone.

Almost.

—Have we lost him then?

—Almost.

## VIII

## THE ORCHARD AND THE FISHERY

Let's laugh with him now, as sometimes happens when he's fed up with forever feeling sad in the same way.

To circumcision I said he is attached—as Saint Augustine to the *felix culpa*. They are attached to the fault, for ultimately there is some good in it, Saint Augustine is attached to the *sin* he committed as Jacques Derrida is attached to the sin committed against him, here a slight difference in reading, the Catholic and the Jewish like a slight sexual difference—touching and drawing apart. The main thing is for the sinning to occur so as to beget the Bible, the cycle of *Confessions*, and thence all of literature.

Sin must have its original scene: wherever a man falls who may be a woman as well, there is a *garden* or a flower-strewn meadow, or *fishery*. The setting of the *Culpa* that brings with it both alliance and exclusion, and the whole history of the world, is forever the same. Adam falls among the flowers of sinning, pear trees for Saint Augustine. Roland falls in the Pyrenees in the middle of a meadow whose flora is sprinkled with his blood, when little Stendhal so harshly sins at the age of five the flowers of the field are daisies, when it's pretty Cherubino who falls, the garden window overlooks a melon bed; and for Stavrogin the crime goes with geraniums. For Jackie, first of all there is the vineyard, and quite as early on, the fishery. As one might expect his fault is immediately divided, enfolded, and multi-plied, he wants to draw out all the evil, all the juice of the evil "that my writing is drawn, withdrawn and drawn out from" he confesses *still without avowal* in period 46, he doesn't stop turning around the evil of evil he makes his honey, honey [*mi-el*] half her [*mi-elle*] no doubt, for better and for worse evil is his good, he never hides from it, which doesn't mean that he boasts of it nor that he flaunts it, but that, if evil pursues him he will let himself be read to the quick by sin, knowing full well period 9 said, very early in the book, that "writing only has interest in proportion to and in the experience of evil." "Has interest" for whom? or what? Has interest for the one who writes the one who reads the one for whom evil is the fount of happiness, *in proportion* he says. The more evil there is the more there is cause and source of writing *in order to ask for pardon.* The more one asks for pardon the more one writes to ask for pardon the more one pardons oneself for writing, the more one conjugates pardons with perjures, the more one writes the more one pardonjures the more one conjures the more one capi-talizes on the most desirable and unpardonable desirable: the taste for writ-ing, more precisely in his own words: "the taste (lost) for holding the pen, for writing well." Thus begins his hymn to voluptuousness, to the volup-tuousness of writing, writs, and scriptures. And to each his own taste. Each taste has its cost and its color, and its dolor also. His—his taste—it should be analyzed at length one day—being composed of loss (by which he means *perte* and *perdre*) of sea [*mer*] and mother [*mère*], of uncircumcised sons, of nostalgia, of regret, of bitterness and all of it mixed together, with a dash of ML, the letters of the sacred words, ML of mohel, ML of the marrow [*moelle*] word of the word Circumcision,—mixed together to make a musi-cal composition fragrant with the unpardonable. He revels in the *Unpardonable.* And no unpardonable of course without desire without *par* without *don* [gift] without *donnable* [givable] without all the ungraspable particles of the dream of pardon. PRD, the letters of PaRaDise. He writes to keep (the memory, the forgetting, the secret) the lost pardon, the *Pardon perdu*. Mindful that each time he writes he loses it all over again and to an even greater extent. A tragic and delicious increase of the fertile fault. But that's what writing is: taking the pen to increase the pain. So he writes the crime [*il écrime*]. And does it again. *Circumfession* avows and as quickly forgets its avowal in order to reavow and revive the avowal with its inexhaustible facets and figures. He reconsiders his avowal, his crime, his avowal as crime-written-down, as if he hadn't yet committed it hadn't properly commenced. He gives us one variation on the first voluptuous theft in period 31 only to play it differently in periods 41, 42, 47, in every one of them in sum since as "*Montaigne would say*," he says at the beginning of period 38 "I am forever disowning myself," he says coming after and playing at Montaigne in his turn, "it is impossible to follow in my tracks" he declares, he himself can't keep up, he loses track, his track can't keep up with him, the morsel he spit up he starts to spit up again, he falls into trances of which he is the enchanted scribe. As for me, I shall examine only one or two of his many tracks, drawn at random, number 31—and number 47. It is in period 31, an analytical and poetic marvel, that the funniest of his sleights of hands is first celebrated: from circumcision, a *sin* he says committed against his will, to the sin replayed that he calls: *autofellocircumcision* a masterpiece of a polyglot compound word. Follow me, this way to the fishery, you are going to die laughing, in Algerire—

The scene: Jackie, at customs, declares his *impossible homosexuality*. Like any guilty party he stutters and speaks of homo-mo-hel-sexuality, he's really impossible!

He gives the name of his partner in homohelsexuality and, as you know, it's Claude Claude, Cl Cl Claude he says, the luck of the name and a lucky name, Claude in French clodhops between masculine and feminine. Now you see it, now you don't. A pass, a pass key of a name. And this fantastic, circumsuspect confession: my impossible homosexuality. He only likes the impossible, so he told us. Impossible doesn't mean impossible, don't you know, impossible to be doubled up. Listen to him tell us about it, doubled up laughing, and laughing [*rire*] doubled up gives us pleasure [*plais-ir*],— keep your eye on the Ri-ir, every letter of it.

❖ ❖ ❖ ❖ ❖ ❖ ❖ ❖ ❖

There you see him acting all the parts, full of zest, reveling in it, to the point of circumcising himself, what a feat, the baby is itself the mohel, the old circumciser, the word [*mot*]—*elle*—the mohelic brat, he's amazing with his penis in one hand, knife in the other. He snips his foreskin, he sucks his own bloody glans with a mouthful of Algerian rosé—he drinks the wine the blood lyre in one hand knife in the other, everything at once. Delirious? No. Stolen pleasure, pleasure is always stolen, it is always the given of a forbidden action, the fault bears fruit, the fruit if one manages to steal it bears fruit in turn, these grapes for example, this bunch of grapes, a sign that weds, in a mischievous masonry, Genet and Claude-and-me all those who get caught with their hand in the bag. Or on the bunch.

(An aside: the lyre here is the penis pincer the surgical instrument that he calls a lyre, he makes music with torture.)

This autofellocircumcision, *coin of a new concept* he says in English, handing us *fellow* along with fellah, in one word, ten words and twenty winks, for clearly the English *fellow*, that typically English bloke, is quite untranslatable by "camarade" or "copain"—less by "complice" this chap who *lays* his *fee*, who puts down his money with the other's—yes the *fellow* companion, before turning into the *bedfellow*, starts by sharing money, then promptly becomes the one who shares everything with another. What have you got to declare? My impossible homosexuality, my autohomohelsexuality, my hand on the bunch, the grapes of my unreason, my madness, and especially my delight in writing this sentence not only for its value, its meaning its truth its actuali-

ty, but because, in its syntactical and lexical powers, it has economic potential. Sneaky. Jewsneaky.

It's the jolt of the potential that makes us burst out laughing. O mo hel!
O my thief! O my theft! I love you. *O meum furtum*, as Saint Augustine says,
O my theft! O my beloved! As he said O my God, O my beloved. Here we
could write a book about Jacques Derrida as robber of himself. From himself
he steals it all and catches himself red-handed. He broadcasts his seed, throws
himself off the track, delights in giving himself the slip. Even his letters.
Even his *foreskin*. Even his thievery. His seed.

He is forever wanting to lay a hand on the bunch of grapes, and get
caught in the act, it escapes him, the bunch, the letters, stolen, found, ripe to
write about. "Since then I have followed the confessions of theft at the heart
of autobiographies." So let us follow in his tracks. Let's follow the marauder's
trail in the tracks of his predecessors in fateful predation. Rousseau's "Un
petit ruban couleur de rose et argent déjà vieux" remains for eternity and as
we shall see, astonishingly, in almost all the texts, a pinkish insistence I leave
to your interpretation: such is reality's or thievery's gift to literature. *Il est rose,*
we are in the pink. Rose is the color of theft in Genet, and rose too the equivocal masculine feminine word, *le* rose (color) and *la* rose (flower). Rose-pink
everywhere in such a way as to make word and thing equivalent to the first
fruit. Which little by little, since Genesis, has been imbued with color. It was
*fruit*, it has been colored, gold yellow orange. There you have the range of the
seductive: gold or pink is the desirable object *accessible inaccessible* (to match
the accessory). Objects one can help oneself to insofar as they are detachable.
There is therefore an appearance of inaccessibility, one can lay hands on them,
as Jacques Derrida says of the bunch of grapes, or as one sees Genet doing
with Stilitano's grapes in the *Journal du voleur*. One can grab them one can
grip them, one can latch on to them, one can *cling to* them. But no matter how
accessible they are, or *because they are accessible*, they are by the same token
inaccessible, no sooner stolen than they escape us, or we escape them. A high-

er police authority turns up to stand in the way of the clinging and the gripping. He who comes along to block: a figure comparable to the narrator's father in *La Recherche du temps perdu*, who is himself a reproduction of Chateaubriand's father figure in the *Mémoires d'outre-tombe*. A most formidable and derisory policeman father with a long phallic cap pulled low over his brow and a candle stuck in his fist. In period 31 of *Circumfession* it is a double, even triple figure, it's the landowner's-guardian-who-is-about-to-call-the-police. A metonymy of intervening authority, it shifts, it doubles and triples, you can peal it like an onion, this character whom Imre Hermann calls the *Reviler* (in *Filial Instinct*, a superb epic of shame), the one who makes you feel ashamed. Thus the Arab landowner in the scene of the successful or unsuccessful theft. Is a theft ever successful or unsuccessful? That is the question. If it's a theft à la Saint Augustine or à la Genet, it is successful since the object is not the theft but the *aura of the theft;* this aura is intangible, but it integrates the body of the thief in the form of all the emotions, all the tremors that he seeks to enjoy. It may look like a gesture of appropriation, but the theft does not satisfy the fantasy of appropriation, on the contrary it makes what is proper shudder in every way.

To come back to the Grapes. We have all had the experience described by La Fontaine in *The Fox and the Grapes*, a ravishing trifle. (Now there's a fable that must elude translation. Everything is stolen in translation. I don't mean that the original text is not stolen, it is stolen that goes without saying [*cela vole de soi*]. Everything written is stolen. The moment one enters into writing, one is in translation, one is translated as one is indicted [*traduit en justice*], one indicts oneself, one steals oneself away, one disappropriates oneself, and one disappropriates the reader to infinity. I am not therefore saying that there is something proper which is the original. There is nothing proper, but there are effects due to the power of a theft that are more striking right up close to the original than from a distance of successive translations.)

THE FOX AND THE GRAPES

One Gascon fox, whom others call Norman
Nearly dead of hunger, spots high on the trellis
A bunch of grapes, ripe in appearance
And sheathed in vermilion skin.
The brigand would gladly have made a meal of them,
But since they were out of his reach:
They are too green, says he, good only for goys

Now was this not better than complaint?

Fables have a body and a soul. The body is the story, and then the envoi, the moral, that's the soul, or so they say. What can be said about this fox? Well, he's . . . Jewish! We shall demonstrate this to you in a moment: Gascon and Norman, from the start he's neither fish nor fowl. Part southern Gascon, part northern Norman. A Gascon promise, as the saying goes. Gascons (according to naively racist stereotypes) are incurable braggarts. And Normans? It's the Norman answer, neither here nor there. When the fox enters, he's undecided, undecidable, if he's Gascon, he's going to lunge at the bunch of grapes even way up over there, but others say he's Norman, quite the opposite, he himself doesn't know. "Grapes ripe in appearance," one sees what he's getting at. "The brigand would gladly have made a meal of them," he would have eaten grapes, even if they weren't fit for a fox. "But since they were out of reach:" here's where we enter the "Jewish" world. All the Talmudic wisdom turns up: if you can't get the grapes, *tell yourself* they are green. I'm making this up? On the other hand I didn't invent: " *et bons pour des goujats,*" not ripe they are good only for *goys*. *Goy*, a Hebrew word, which has come into American English through Yiddish, in the mouth of "Jews" designates the not-good, the not-Jewish. A word that has got around as few words have, from: *goya*, a word from the langue d'oc, which means servant, valet, someone of little worth, a good-for-nothing, a boor, a rustic lout. Our word has come down, gone back up, taken a grand tour round Europe and come back via the Germanic in order to cross to the United States at long last. It's good for those who are loutish, and not one of us. And there you have our Jewish fox, a terrific gift from La Fontaine, who tells us something about the way we see or judge the grapes according to whether they are accessible or not, pickable or not, grabbable or not. You can't get the grapes? They are good for goys.

The grapes bring me back to the bunch of Derrida cousins and to the world of childhood as in this mystery: where does the child begin, where does the child finish? And presto here's Jacques Derrida as Cherubino! In the place of the kid's cap I give him Suzanne's bonnet. Is this a child? What is a child? Girl or boy? Fish or fowl? Fig or grape? That's the question *The Marriage of Figaro* asks of Cherubino. A big question that shook its epoch, a question Beaumarchais went after. In a brilliant *preface* he described the adventures of what he had called *The Mad Day* or *The Marriage of Figaro* with the censors. This play was censored, put off, rendered inaccessible to the public for years by a whole series of censors, like a mouthwatering bunch of grapes. As always, in any country in which there is censorship, in which the accusation does not show its face but proceeds entirely by insinuation. And Beaumarchais couldn't stop turning over the various reasons for which the play might have been censored for so long, before being set free by the actors themselves. A wonderful story like the story of theater itself. He lingers over it, and over the character of Cherubino, for as he says *"could it be the character that so scandalizes you: is it my page who shocks you?"* Or is it my page? The scandal, the *skandalon*, is the stumbling block, the thing that trips you up. Cherubino is not a rolling stone, he's a flying stone.

Is it my page that so scandalizes you, and might the immorality one blames at the base of the work, be in the accessory, in what is secondary?

Is *the immorality in the accessory*, in what is secondary? "Accessory," an ambiguous word that speaks of all the accessories: the secondary (which is not secondary; it seconds, backs up); the theatrical accessory or prop: the play revolves around Cherubino "the accessory," it *runs on Cherubino*: the motor of this play, the one who oversees all its tricks: who pulls all the strings and ribbons. A superb word *accessory*: it comes from the Latin *accessorius*, from *accedere*, which speaks of the *junction*, the *joint*. That's what Cherubino is: the one who joins all the manners in the play. There is no joint that is not disjointed. *The mad day* is a *disjointed day*, completely *out of joint*. Now it just so happens that it is a wedding day. How to form an alliance in a world whose every joint is coming unstuck, which is dislocated like a puppet? The play is endangered in every joint, and up to the very last second, one has no idea whether it will manage to conjoin in holy matrimony. But isn't marriage a promise of disjunction? Cherubino is the incarnation of this assemblage of joint-disjoint, the coming apart, the unscrewing, the genie and the *angel of the clinging*. *Cheruban: cheribbon.*

I'm going to let that go for a moment. Let's take a little detour to the garden of El-Biar, in the suburbs of Algiers. It will be mini-fig, mini-grape. Here we see Jacques Derrida doff Cherubino's bathing costume and don Ali-Baba's turban.

13, rue d'Aurelle-de-Paladines, El-Biar, it's still the orchard, the intact PaRDeS, the seamless present that continues you, the imperturbable phenomenon that you will never see age, you no longer grow old, although everything is decided in this garden, and the law, as far as memory extends, the death of two children, Jean-Pierre Derrida, the cousin, one year older than you, knocked down by a car in front of his home in Saint-Raphaël, at school they tell you your brother has died, you believe it, a moment of annihilation from which you have never recovered, and five years later, 1940, the death of Norbert Pinhas, your little brother this time, 2 years old, then expulsion from the high school and from Frenchness, damnation games with Claude, Claude and Claudie, kissing cousins, so many stolen figs, at the origin is theft and perjury, on the eve of Ali Baba's 59 secrets, one undecipherable secret per jar, on each date a drop of blood, one date suffices to leave the geologic program behind, like the drop you saw well up on the back of the little girl allowing herself distractedly to be buggered, scarcely, with gestures that are sure but as gauche as those of the mammal being born, she knows you've got a hard-on on your father's bed, turned . . .

There we have the orchard's address: "13, rue d'Aurelle-de-Paladines, El-Biar" Derrida's address in El-Biar, the address of his orchard, "of my intact PaRDeS," of Aurelle-de-Paladines, an illustrious nobody, general of the Empire. For in Algeria the streets and boulevards were subjected to colonization, a highly insidious extension of the empire of the proper. "It's still the orchard," this is a text written in at least four times, Derrida has said, as there are at least four rabbis, etc. One notes also the typographical winks, for example the "intact PaRDes." This is the written Paradise, the Paradise of before vowels. These four consonants, PRDS, contain a Talmudic reference.

Talmudic hermeneutics are too infinite for me to venture into them here. I shall only in all earthly humility recall the link between the *Pardes* and reading: the Pardes as garden of reading or, as we would say Jacques Derrida and I in memory of the marvelous garden of Algiers, as *Garden of essays*. Biblical interpreters in effect employed four methods of exegesis designated by the four consonants of the word *pardes*. They were *peshat* (simple), literal interpretation; *remez* (allusion), allegorical interpretation; *derach* (exposition), homiletical commentary; *sod* (mystery), esoterical teaching.

Number 13, rue d'Aurelle-de-Paladines, one may or may not recognize the following thieves, that is, those who precede Jacques Derrida, pell-mell Augustine, Rousseau, Adam and Eve, Ali Baba and his forty pickpockets, and here too, once again, the clan of the Cls, Clau-Clau-Clau-of-die, we are in period 47, in the Sesame cavern, in the paternal bedroom, 13, rue d'Aurelle-de-Paladines, El-Biar: *the 13th comes back*, it is still the first room, the bed, the hour of the theft, Aurelia, and it is always the same. One sees how one mustn't omit from the list of robbers and robbed, other intertextualized authors surreptitiously mentioned among whom (quick wink at French school culture, the "Frenchness" from which he was expelled), pass, effaced, even Gerard de Nerval, another of those dreamers of Paradise lost. Number 13, rue d'Aurelle-de-Paladines, writes a version, disguised to the point of unrecognizability, of the love of Aurelia or some other "distracted" little girl; who'd have believed it [*qui l'eût crue*]? And yet. It must be read crude [*lu cru*]: let us stop time here as the *suspension of the present* in this period suggests and, in this arrestation of the "still," read on.

❖ ❖ ❖ ❖ ❖ ❖ ❖ ❖ ❖ ❖ ❖

*Intact*, says period 47, craftily "the *intact* PaRDeS": right away one opens the textual bag of tricks. It is bottomless. To begin with Paradise has an address, although Talmudists and esotericians have endless discussions concerning its whereabouts, what address to write him at? He has innumerable addresses, just as there are innumerable dates for the coming of the Messiah. So why not "13, rue d'Aurelle-de-Paladines"? Second wink, "it's still the orchard," he could have said garden, he chose orchard [*verger*] for the penis (*verge*) and the rods [*verges*]: he who lays hand on the penis will be struck by the rod. "The *intact* PaRDeS" is said to be located in El-Biar. This address opens an immense orchard or garden of contradictory meditations. Is Paradise intact, is *intact* that which has not been touched, that which is whole, virgin?

Jacques Derrida speaks of the *intact paradise*, whereas everything in this period says the contrary, is about tact, touch, violent touch, scarcely about circumcision, about laying a hand on, about grabbing. The ideal paradise, the one we have lost, was the one that was intact, where one hadn't touched, where Adam and Eve, newborn mammals, had not touched the tree of good and evil; must one enter here another paradise where something is never to be touched, or hardly, the green [*vert*], hence not yet wholly perverse, paradise of childish loves? Perhaps, however it is handled, the essence of this paradise remains intact immutable, and in its sublime form, perhaps in its esoteric form, it escapes touch that nonetheless touches it? "The seamless present that continues you," the theme is the same, the present being that which we never have access to, which would be seamless, whereas we are forever in the seams or folds of time. "The imperturbable," this is the paradigmatic ensemble of all that is untouched and that remains inalterable, like you [*tu*] it doesn't grow old. The reverse of all we have learned. Before the fall Adam and Eve were virgins, even if they'd had sexual relations, and they did not grow old. Here is Paradise reestablished at the stroke of a pen. I also note the bent of the personal pronoun: "the seamless present that continues you [*tu*], the imperturbable phenomenon that you will never see age, you no longer grow older." He says *tu* (you) because in Jacques there are two people: *je*, the one who grows old while *tu* no longer grows old. Right to the very end: "*I* am sure *you* look like him, you look more and more like your mother." Throughout this period there is a double subject, the *tu* subject and the *je* subject, with an enallage of person, this sort of very slight slippage whereby *you* takes the place of *I* who takes his place again later, out of restlessness or faithfulness to Derrida's thought, which is a thought about substitution. There is no *I* that is not several, often *I* is yesterday's *you*, or on the contrary it is today's *you*, the seamless present that continues you. On the one hand he is kept forever young over there in El-Biar he continues, on the other he is the one who is writing in four times, not only in 89 and 99, but also in 77, as in 2789, simultaneous dates, dates we can call dates, like the fruit. This time the stolen pleasure is not grapes, it is not the hand on the bunch of grapes, but "the damnation games with Claude, Claude and Claudie." The names that have been associated with the "impossible homosexuality" since period 31. Claude, an undecidable name, who signs Claude? Fig or grape? One does not know who Claude Claude is *claudius claudicus*, the one who limps in Latin; one never knows which way to turn with Claude, or which way Claude turns. Which way to turn him-her, whereupon Jacques Derrida sweeps us off to paradise with his damnation music. The damnation games can only take place in paradise, the paradise must be stolen. "Claude, Claude and Claudie, kissing cousins [*cousins cousines*]": no punctuation between *cousin* and *cousines*, the *cousins* are *cousines* and the *cousines* are *cousins*. And how many Claudes in Claude? One and two, or one, two, or three? May the undecidable decide. Back to the top: "you no longer grow older, although everything is decided in this garden": in *jardin* the accent is on *jar*, will *jar*din decide? It goes with *jar*, and *par jarre*, per jar, goes with *parjure*, to perjure. Nothing has been decided in this garden, but "everything is decided," this is where it all begins, where everything is sent for deciding and cutting up, "and the law, as far as memory extends, the death of two children, Jean-Pierre Derrida, the cousin, one year older than you, knocked down by a car." An automobile (1940's vocabulary) "in front of his home in St. Raphaël" (this Arab land is chockablock with names of saints and French generals), "at school they tell you your brother has died, you believe it, a moment of annihilation from which you have never recovered." At this point, he is dead, dead from the death of his brother, who is not dead, because it's his cousin, at least not yet, it's "five years later, the death of Norbert Pinhas, your little brother this time," does he believe it this time? that he is dead from the death of his little brother, 13, rue d'Aurelles-de-Paladines, El-Biar. Memory, at least, has two times: that which does not budge, which remains in the garden, it is no longer him in the garden, but in his place there is you; and then the return to a present in which the past is lost. " . . . your little brother this time, 2 years old, then expulsion from high school and from Frenchness" (the Vichy period). "Damnation games with Claude, Claude and Claudie, kissing cousins, so many stolen figs, in the beginning is theft and perjury, just before the 59 secrets of Ali Baba, one undecipherable secret per jar," "so many stolen figs" remains undecidable. A kind of fruit that is not a fruit, that's what kissing cousins steal. He doesn't tell the sex of the fruit here. But a little further on (in case we weren't sure) "a drop of blood . . . wells up . . . like the one you saw . . . on the back of the little girl allowing herself distractedly to be buggered, scarcely, with gestures that are sure but as gauche as those of a mammal being born," we don't know who buggers, who makes the sure gestures, "she knows you've got a hard-on on your father's bed, turned toward the radio . . . " read aloud the difference is troubling, hearing it one doesn't know who is turned toward the radio, it could be the bed, it could be the father, it could be him, it could be the little girl. Derrida doesn't *tell* us, he *writes it. Writing, however, is not telling. The key of* Circumfession is precisely that: *what is written is not said.* Never in his life would Derrida say such a thing, never in his life would he be caught in a "confession" scene. Never will he be caught in a *Catholic* situation, he is not Catholic, there will never be a confession. This is not a confession, it is a circumfession, it's written, not said. "So many stolen figs," one doesn't know by whom, what, how, but damnation says all that: in paradise there's what happens, "at the origin of everything," of all thought of all history of all writing, "is theft and perjury, just before the 59 secrets of Ali Baba." The fifty-nine periods, these fifty-nine years, which are also "59 secrets" or fifty-nine jars full of secrets, fifty-nine secrets therefore fifty-nine thieves and fifty-nine victims of robbery. We are not to know what the secrets are. When the time comes *to write the secrets he only writes them and doesn't tell them.* There he is as Ali Baba "one undecipherable secret per jar," playing at perjury. The perjuries remain in the jar guarded by Ali Baba. " . . . on each date a drop of blood, one date suffices to leave the geologic program behind": Jeff Bennington's computer program, its ambitious game of indexing the totality of Jacques Derrida's thought, all of Derrida precooked and served up, to which Jacques Derrida answers: he's going to program the whole of my unconscious, all my work, and at the same time a single date, one secret date will blow the whole thing up. " . . . at each date a drop of blood . . . like the one you saw well up on the back of the little girl." Then a Latin quotation from Saint Augustine: "*Numquid mentior aut mixtione misceo neque distinguo lucidas cognitiones harum rerum in firmamento caeli et opera corporalia* (Do I lie? Do I bring confusion by not distinguishing the clear knowledge of these things in the firmament of heaven from the bodily works?)" So at the very moment he writes this scene of buggery for us, along comes Augustine who denies it in Latin: perhaps I am lying to you, perhaps you believed it was real, but perhaps it was a phantasm. In Latin, *are you with me?* Or maybe you are lost? That tease of a little girl. It was *you*, dear reader, who was being mocked.

"that means . . . that you never write like SA," SA in place of Saint Augustine, but also as abbreviation of the word *signifier* and homophone of *ça*, the id. You'll never get to the bottom of it.

"You never write like SA, the father of Adeodat whose mother is nameless" (Adeodat's) father is Saint Augustine, who is no longer designated save by the name of his son, Adeodat, whom he loves infinitely, whom he bears along with him in the wake of his different conversions, and who dies in the end. Saint Augustine nameless; reduced; father of a named son. But if the son has a name, the son's mother (and not Augustine's lover) has never had one. Derrida gives Saint Augustine back his own; you do not name Adeodat's mother, therefore you too for once shall be nameless, you are to be designated by the antonomasia "father of Adeodat". No he never writes like the father of Adeodat whose mother is nameless, for him the mother is not nameless.

"They are too *marranos*, too 'Catholic,' they would have said in the rue d'Aurelle-de-Paladines," *a private joke* [in English in the text] they called it in

Algerian Jewish society. "Too far from the orchard, they say discourse" and not they write the text, "like the sign of circumcision, external *or* internal." This is the great difference between the spoken, the uttered, and the written, between the internal or external signs. He, however, has "more than two languages, the figural and the other, and there are at least 4 rabbis, at least" and a great many more than that . . .

## The ribbon is rose

Let us return now to our ribbon, this surprising tie that runs through our texts. And that links *Circumfession* and Rousseau's *Confessions*, not just the confession theme, nor that of the impossible avowal but, even more powerfully invested by the unconscious, the question of *colors*, and the primal scenes that engender these immense works.

The ribbon is pink, rosy pink. It can only be pink.

The ribbon this *ringband*, twice-telling the tie, the ring, was originally a neck-tie, made of a thin strip of fabric. *Ring* + *band* begins to be necklace, then it takes to running all around the body, attaching itself here and there, as befits its ribbony nature, yards and yards of ribbon to cut. Before arriving on or near us, before being the *accessory*, and joining up with a piece of clothing in one way or another, it is first of all interminably cut up, this ribbon subject to continuity discontinuity, this ribbon is pink. See it in Chardin's paintings so often embellished with neck ribbons, sometimes slender as threads, at others wider, the ribbon is pink.

The ribbon is always pink.

See it flow like a ferret through *The Marriage of Figaro*. The ribbon is the *countess's* because it needs the *count*, there are always counts or accounts in our stories of ribbons. Madame de Vercellis's heir is a count. The countess is *Rosine. The Mad Day*, which ought to bring about the marriage of Figaro and

Suzanne, is designed as a round of servants above whom the count and countess's circle revolves. Leaping and bounding like the story's pet monkey, Cherubino the countess's nephew and godson, is poised between the different levels of society. Between their beds as well. He turns up in the bed of Suzanne's little niece Fanchette, the little girl buggered by the little boy, he turns up at Suzanne's, at the countess's, up a tree or down in a bed of melons, this Cherubino now a girl now a lieutenant and always himself—*toujours cher ruban*—:

> CHERUBINO: Oh, Suzanne! I would give . . . what have you got there?
> SUZANNE, *mocking*: Alas! the happy nightcap and the lucky ribbon that
>    bind the hair of your lovely godmother at night . . .

Close-up on the metonymy, it is a happy nightcap, oh, that I should be the lucky ribbon.

> CHERUBINO, *keenly*: The ribbon she wears at night! Give it to me, my
>    heart.
> SUZANNE, *pulling it back*: Oh! what's this "his heart"! How familiar he
>    is! If it weren't an inconsequential young puppy . . .

It's like the stolen figs, there is already reason enough, but it's of no consequence.

(*Cherubino snatches the ribbon.*) Ah, the ribbon!

And the ribbon race is off.

> CHERUBINO [CHERUBON] *circling around the big armchair*: You can say
>    you misplaced it, ruined it; that it's lost. Say what you like.

Isn't this Rousseau's ribbon, misplaced lost spoiled old, etc.

SUZANNE, *running after him*: Oh! in three or four years I predict that
    you will be the biggest little good-for-nothing! . . . Are you going
    to give my ribbon back?

*She tries to take it.*

CHERUBINO: Give it, oh, do let me keep it, Suzanne . . .

Cherubino-ribbon was expelled from little Fanchette's, on whom he had
lavished every possible caress, by the count-*reviler*. Why does the count stop
Cherubino flirting with Fanchette? Because the count is still *in place*, it's the
substitution waltz. Don Almaviva wants even little Fanchette? It is well and
truly a matter of course, place, and substitution, but says Beaumarchais's
preface, at length and magnificently, with comic, necessary, and political bad
faith: he's only a child. The whole sexuality question comes in here, he is only
thirteen, how can the count accuse a child of thirteen of always being in the
place, in the bed, in the sheets, of encroaching on the count's rights, whose
flowerbeds won't plump up after all? How to accuse a thirteen-year-old little
boy of being the root of the scandal?

    This exchanging, which goes on at all times, bring us up to the present.
What is masculine, feminine sexuality, what is sexuality? All women are
cheruribboned or cherubinical. When Beaumarchais pleads against censorship, he is addressing men. He is on the side of women. The women are on
his side. In the end the political and sexual scene always eludes judgment, it
holds the very secret of eroticism.

    The count, an adult, virile, macho male, runs after all the women, who
all reject him. He who was the seducer in *The Barber of Seville*, in passing from
one play to the other, becomes impotent. And there we have a treatise on sex-

uality, in the form of a comedy; Beaumarchais pleads the difference between comedy and tragedy. Everything that is possible in tragedy, he says, is forbidden in comedy, and this is perfectly true. Comedy is the mirror of society: in it people refuse to tolerate anything that might cause ridicule, whereas any crime is tolerable, so long as it is presented in tragic form.

But, to return to our ribbon story, bonnet ribbon, ribbon stolen from a painting of Chardin or Fragonard, it is going to run through the entire castle, a round trip that will bring it back from thief Cherubino (but not such a thief as all that, since he has accomplices, the ribbon lets itself be stolen, the beribboned let themselves be robbed, the ribbon takes a grand tour of every scene and closet) to the countess only too pleased to be robbed. Cherubino clings to the countess, his adored she-monkey—the story starts with his expulsion, but he is still there! as the count exclaims he returns in all his guises, under every dress, in every color, as for the ribbon, it finds its way back to the countess, the countess takes the (dear) ribbon back, which in the meantime has soaked up Cherubino's libido, and in extremis, but it's a long story, she takes the ribbon back and keeps it safe in her bosom. Meanwhile the ribbon has acquired all sorts of virtues, it heals, it is magic obviously, carrier of everything a "well-tempered" eroticism engenders. As for the child with his variable sex, the ribbon-bounder, neither reason nor force nor the police nor shame about which he doesn't care a fig can do anything about his propensity to cling : quite the contrary reprisals and interruptions feed his voluptuousness. Cherubino can't go away, even if the count to shake him off makes a man of him, offers him the masculine insignia, his commission (which he promptly loses) as a *lieutenant* (*sic*) in the company of which he is the colonel. The colonel tries in vain to make importunate eros go away, *by promoting him*. But the potency by way of the erection is not to be found in the promotion. The accessory jumps out the window and scampers right back to the countess's bosom. Members of the monkey clan communicate by clinging, by itching and scratching gestures. The process that gathers together and allies all monkey characters is a gesture of detachment: picking lice, plucking hairs, peeling off skin. In unity detachment. As if clinging and loss of clinging were being repeated in this familiar and religious scene. The countess is a former Cherubino. She perpetuates the lost clinging with Cherubino. It is difficult for her to say I am an ex-Cherubino or old young monkey. And yet she says it, in monologues, not telling anyone, except the entire audience. But the audience doesn't exist. What is secondary is most powerful. What counts is not the main action, it is what is secondary: it is the running, the pursuit, the interminable desire, the metonymic machine, and not the action. The charm of *The Marriage of Figaro* is the opposition, incredibly true to life, between two sorts of sexuality: that which *takes action*, the count's, flickers out; while that which is in hot pursuit of the ribbon is still crackling. The reviler, count, ember-eyed father who would like to force the baby monkey to loosen its grip on the she-monkey merely reinforces its urge to cling. Beaumarchais, a marvelous precursor of Imre Hermann! And of Jacques Derrida as well: but in this case the coincidence is less obvious. And yet, and yet . . .

He too holds passionately to, is held by, a snippet of pink ribbon, *déjà vieux*. Which is to say, very, very old and stolen or flitting around. He too traverses castles, gardens, books, now joining up with Genet now with Rousseau unless it be with SA so as to enjoy what makes him suffer. But if the grapes and other sorts of fruit are edible and replaceable, the ribbon is unique. As we have seen. It is the ring of the foreskin, the ribbon of pink flesh, stolen, the legend goes, with the help of the mother. Will it ever come back? One should expect it to turn up—concealed under some disguise, bonnet, cap, turban, bathing costume . . .

The theater: it is always PRDS. The characters: always the quivering band of pals, scamps, cherubinos, undecidable children. Those objects of desire I call the accessories.

The *accessories,* or props, without which there would be no story, drama, no literature, are the secret genies of the soul's Theater, from Othello's hand-kerchief to Rousseau's ribbon, the accessories are the occult masters of our tragedies.

The accessories in the El-Biar PRDS: figs, grapes; pears for Augustine; pinkribbon for Jean-Jacques; pinkribbon for Cherubino. One can lose one's soul to such accessories. But what's in a (pink) ribbon? What is a (pink) rib-bon? A fig? Or bunch of grapes? And to the list of famous stolen objects I add: the foreskin. What does thief Augustine tells us about his experience? I stole for the sake of stealing, I wasn't stealing the pears, besides they were fit for pigs. Therefore surely not for the race of Arabs, Berbers, of which Augustine was a member, he who appropriated desired not the solid fruit, but something behind the fruit in the fruit, and that is bravado, the challenge. What he wished to savor was the juice of a challenge, and in particular a chal-lenge to the law, to authority. That plus something else, with his circle of Claudes, the *pals*. Thievery on the fringes of cities began with Saint Augustine, and probably with Saint Augustine's ancestors, the great-great-grandparents of those ruffian gangs, whose joy is *to band together* trading, mak-ing deals, alliances, pacts, thanks to some ordinary stolen object, for the pleasure of breaking the law. Others go after figs or grapes, without really knowing what it is they are stealing. Neither fish nor fowl, a little fig, a lit-tle grape, one hardly knows what one is after, am I with the figs or with the grapes, or somewhere in between, am I with the bunch or on the other hand with the fig? Or with the figrape? *Fig*: fruit that is not fruit in the botanical sense of the term but that is a pyriform receptacle, pear-shaped, fruit-bearing. *Faire la figue*, an obscene gesture, in today's French *faire la nique*, to thumb your nose. *Mi-figue mi-raisin*, neither here nor there, ambiguous, feminine masculine, we do not know how they connect, cluster, or on the contrary come apart, these bisexualities or androgynies rampant in our trees. Between the fig (or the grape), from fruit that is more than one fruit and bears fruit, and Rousseau's ribbon, there is continuity. For the ribbon, as Rousseau himself writes, bore fruit for its (un)fortunate robber: all of Rousseau's work is the fruit of this distressing period.

(I'm not forgetting, even if I don't take time to go into it here, that before the theft of the ribbon there was the splendid episode of the apple stolen through a *jalousie* in the *dispensary* of Monsieur Verrat, the proprietor named for a pig . . . And before the theft of the apple there was the theft of water, and before that theft, there was the theft . . . But Rousseau himself dated his entry into dis-simulation by writing the crime committed for the sake of the *ruban rose déjà vieux.*)

And the foreskin, ring, ribbon of pink flesh, stolen, so they say, with the help of the mother, cut off the son, where oh where has it gone?

# IX

## SECOND SKIN

*In the armoire*, here it is in Hebrew in its transfigure, *the tallith*, "it waits for me tucked away in its hiding place at home, it never travels." In place of the stolen skin, this other, the hidden skin, not from just any animal but from the sheep the ewe or ram (*Voiles*, p. 67) the commemorative skin, the death-commemorating skin of a ewe that was alive and died for the tallith, the skin that *remembers* the *Korban*, the offering that brings close, the proximate skin, the hypothesis under whose protection he murmurs, no, he keeps murmuring, the prayer shawl, the *shawl* he insists and not the veil, the word shawl introducing an Indian note, the skin, of a ewe perhaps, but for the body and soul of *man*.

Yet another male thing? Reserved? Exclusive? Perhaps but it won't take him long to circumvent masculine law.

Here, under the tent of the tallith, an extraordinary hymn mounts to *she* who waits for him "hidden" in her hiding place at home him forever traveling *she* never voyages. I said *she* yes, not a slip of the tongue, I follow the signs of his.

He says and writes of the tallith that it is unique as you've heard. By means of tallith and tongue he delicately introduces the theme of the liaison. He has a liaison with the tallith that is unique, *qui est unique. Tunic by liaison,* probably his only liaison, one that is weightless, that waits, a skin for his skin, that doesn't capture but protects him, keeps watch over him without keeping him. He loves his tunic and he sings of it in moving accents, caresses himself with it, against her, like a cat, as the cat just barely caresses him, a light touch grazing the skin, he is fonder of it than anything else this masculine feminine thing he calls, this is unique in his language, *my very own tallith*.

All his life he has fought against the veil in the veil's counterdance, dreaming of a lifting of the veil that, so as not to be a mere an unreveiling should, might, come from the other, it's the silkworm's dream to be born of the voice of the other, to be called. Without illusion, without the least figment of a veil over or in back of his eyes. But under no condition, he swears, would he dream of getting rid of the soft pelt of his shawl. Without illusion nonetheless. One doesn't forget there's a dead ram in the Jewish tallith.

But calling it *my-own-tallith* is also a way of setting it apart, of differentiating it from other talliths at least trying to draw it away from the memory of the sacrificial offerings, he has no illusions about what in the Jewish religion is sacrificial, not at all incongruous with the idea of the veil that's how it is there is blood on it, except on mine he would like to believe, the tunic unlike others. And who knows perhaps, *white* as it is, his is the tallith of before all talliths, the pre-original shawl. It suffices to believe, weeping

[no] "theory-of-fetishism" can ever measure up to the infinite compassion that comes from brushing up against, from the caress of a tallith, of my tallith, "my very own tallith." . . . I would like to sing the very solitary softness of my tallith, a softness softer than softness,

Do you remember? My child, my sister, imagine the softness of going to live there together utterly unique, both sensitive and insensitive, calm, acquiescent, a stranger to sensibility, to effusion or pathos, to all "Passion" in short. Boundless compassion, however, a compassion without idolatry, proximity and infinite distance. I love the tranquil passion, the absent-minded love my tallith inspires in me, I feel it allows me this absent-mindedness because it is sure, so sure of me, so little concerned about my infidelities. It doesn't believe in my inconstancies, they don't affect it. I love it and bless it with a strange indifference, my tallith, with a nameless, ageless familiarity. . . . My white tallith belongs to the night, to absolute night. You will never know anything about it, nor I without doubt.

(Voiles, P. 79)

Love with the seeing-eye fingers of the blind, love you feel with the tips of your fingers, with your lips, it's the dream of love, perfect love.

"I touch it without knowing what I do nor what I ask at that moment, and especially without knowing in whose hands I put myself, without knowing to whom I give thanks" (*Voiles*, p. 46). There is no knowing, only grace and thanksgiving there where there is neither knowing nor seeing.

There he is with his Jewish touch, a Jew groping for his tallith, a Jew with an undecided tallith: not knowing, at the end of the wordless grace, of the life so short but so long, with the tunic he loves that loves him, whether he will be ashes or buried in his tallith, letting his loved ones decide.

Yes but I thought he would never give it up no matter what? Doesn't he say:

Right to the very end, never, no matter what: under no circumstances, whatever the verdict at the end of such a redoubtable "*journey*," does one give up a tallith. One must never, at any moment, throw it out or reject it.

(Voiles, P. 68–69)

Yes but after the end?

If there are fire and ashes, then what? I can go no further than the life without violence. I stop without knowing and without seeing. I shall stay with the vision of his astounding union with the white tallith, *this white wedding that belongs to the night.*

We shall never know.

This was the marvelous tale of the Jew of the night. One can only tell it in French, with a French that surpasses French. Just as he goes beyond the French language, so his Jewish being his Jewish not-being [*son n'être juif*] his Jewish birth [*son naître juif*] surpasses (being not being) Judaity Judaism Judaicity Judaica and everything else that might come along with a *j, u,* and *d*, for *if* as a *Marrano* he is Jewish at least it is *in passing*, between the French language*, in the turns* of French, a passer-by.

## The main character of his work is French

From the very beginning, from the playground at school, that's where he met up with his eternal adversary friend interlocutor, *French*. The French language he will have had his whole life to do battle with. In school he likes it when he *has* French. Then explications, arguments, quarrels, hugs, the figures of his impossible homotextuality.

And then, up from under the floorboards—the theatrical ground of this tirade, this *algarade* (from the Spanish *algarada*, from the Arab *al-ghara*)— making themselves heard by the insistent and welcome—caressed even— hosts, elves, and gnomes, come Latin and Greek or perhaps Greek and Latin. A magic nostalgia keeps calling up the two of them his best friends. They (masculine or feminine) are always there, chanted, like a chorus with French as coryphaeus.

French and haunted, French is always speaking to him.

*Le Français* I say. But she whom he adores is *la langue française*. He is wild about her and makes her wild about him. He sits her down on his lap. She tells him her names. His names. Only to him.

As only poets, perhaps only as Rimbaud.

I said of the tallith earlier that it was Hebrew, but immediately afterward as unique tunic, we could hear it was *Hebrew in French*.

Hebrew, he makes no secret of it, for him it's Hebrew or Chinese if you prefer. For him as for me as for my brother, as for so many victims or accomplices of a comfortable acculturation upon which the aforementioned Algerian Jewish community edified its desire for France in the deformation years of the twenties and thirties. Strange autoimmune craze, hence those whose soul was already formed and who had a keen ear for the things of the spirit had a good laugh over it and a great deal of suffering.

We were gripped by a circus feeling. We would see so many of those let's call them "Algerian Jews"—for the sake of brevity—performing their high-wire act in the void. Spangled in French but sporting kippas we called skull-caps, out they swung, having let go of the bar of their old culture, left it far behind them, in Morocco, swimming across the abyss arms reaching out for the other trapeze, the much-desired French, but there's France, hostile, snatching it back. The Jewish trapezists cling to the void. A community out of step with the times. One often spoke a rather elegant French, the language of the denied and oft-flattered enemy. Hebrew? So suppressed. At best one was at the Marrano stage but unaware of it. Humbly my Oran uncles made believe at the dinner table, under the true false skullcap they gabbled away. I admired them: to me they were the last of the faithful or was it just the opposite? Imagine the enormous weight of the word *Jew*, the swelling, the erection of the word, sole survivor of an extinct verbal population.

To think that in the Derrida family they'd naturalized the bar mitzvah, converted it to French. In our house, Cixous-half Klein, Omi kept watch, my German grandmother, French did not do quite the same damage. We said bar mitzvah. But all the same we caught Algeria that disease of autocolonialized communities.

—My bar mitzvah! hoots my brother, what a joke! You had to recite the Shema Israel which is your basic prayer. I was under the arcades on Bab Azoun Street with the rabbi in front of a shitty little synagogue maybe pretty he says. Do you know the Shema? asks the rabbi. The Shema I thought, a shema in the ass! my brother says. Yes, I replied unfazed. So recite it for me. Of course, I exclaimed. I start off. I say Shema Israel Blablablah nice and loud. Fine says the rabbi. He stops me. You can say Shema. Afterward in the tram—after the bar mitzvah—I tell Granny our Oran grandmother with my ritual subtlety risen from the depths of my rage: I hope we're having ham for lunch.

That was 1951. For him it was in 1943 at an Isly Street rabbi's he had to sham.

They would ask these boys my brothers: do you know the Shibboleth, at least a bit of it, hey? It starts with a Shi says the brother. Good says the rabbi. Who will recount the circoncessions of the Isly or Lyre Street rabbis? The main thing is to barmitzvah the boy eyes shut. But don't tell anybody says my mother. She fears the worst sin is not the sin, it's the telling strangers. Some "goy."

The troubled identity, the trouble whereby the tremor passes between us, has also to do with this difficulty of saying, this preaching of not telling, the shame-faced culture unashamed of its lack of culture. But keep it to yourself. Don't tell a soul.

The crime is making believe in bad faith. In those days he hadn't found out about his *marranity*, therefore he was innocent.

How to escape unscathed from a scene in which I take *communion* instead of having my bar mitzvah, what a circummunion! "It's my feast day" he tells himself in French, they feast him, yet another circumcision.

His genius gets the best of these cruel comedies—gives it wings—like
Elie

> I did my "communion" by fleeing the prison of all languages, the
> sacred one they tried to lock me up in without opening me to it, the
> secular they made clear would never be mine, but this ignorance
> remained the chance of my faith as of my hope, of my taste even for the
> "word."
>
> (PERIOD 54)

We were always imposters doubled up in an excruciating laugh. Offended
offenders. My brother and I at Hanukkah bursting out laughing singing *ma
au sau ne chou aussi*, making a mishmash of cabbage and currants and the her-
metic hymn.

Not kosher: conjurers. Jugglers with language, swallowers of the ashes of
words. What remained of Hebrew.

(Here I owe a mark of respect to my father the circumcised atheist: when
I was ten he gave me two teachers one of Arab one of Hebrew. Then he died
and I had my two paternal languages cut off.)

At last *Le Monolinguisme de l'autre* came along to say everything one was
not supposed to say, a splendor of an apocalyptic testimony in a language that
is merciless that owes nothing to anyone, about the plots against the soul,
outrages, interlingual persecutions, the whole war beneath the surface of the
Algerian wars, our daily lot, a history rich in tormentdreams, in battles
between regiments of identificatory phantasms, my grandfather Samuel
Cixous as a Zouave, we always were a strange bunch of Zouaves, the great
book of our terrors tells it all, interrogations, torture, drawn and quartered by
hyphens what does it mean to be a Franco-North African Jew is that something you add on or subtract or maybe you take it away from any attempt at

collective action? Still we ask it and to have to answer, in a language that is Hebrew in French for us, for a belonging constituted of exclusion and non-belonging, what does it mean to be from Algeria not Algerian, Jew by the other, French by decree, disenFrenched by decree, to be constantly decreeicized, furthermore forever not-like, not like the other not like me, subdivided, circumceded, circumdecided, improbable, what is this verb to be, the great persecutor.

Who can say what it is, this Franco-North-African creature Jew-nonetheless or in-spite-of-everything or Jew-who-doesn't-know-that-he-is, how to know who is better placed to know anything, when are Jews Jews in what way I wondered are my mother and her German sister Jewish more Jewish than Russians Jews perforce, "no Jew has ever nor will ever know anything for certain" it seems to me I read that on the ceiling of Montaigne's library but I am not certain of it, the more my mother and her sister seem sure of knowing what is or what is not to be or not to be the more unsettled I am, perhaps it is enough to be *certain* but in what order are they Germans or Jews English or French Jewish or French sometimes German Jews sometimes German French or on the other hand English Jewish with a German passport also Israeli (infinitely Jewisher in their opinion than the forced-to-be synagogue Russians who know nevertheless and know only that they were Jews but one must say that they are not Jews all they know is that they once were).

*Le Monolinguisme de l'autre* tells us everything there is to know about the mental anguish to which we owe our books of memoirs— . . .

For sometimes, as in his case, from malediction comes benediction. We are indebted to certain wounds for the greatest works of art.

Such is this chopped up Jewish "community" that thrice cuts itself off from its language
   1. cut from the Arab and Berber languages
   2. cut from French or even European language and culture

3. cut for—from Jewish memory,

such is this Jewish memory cut off from its memory,

such is the dialogue with his mother 1. that cannot take place 2. that never took place

such is the voyage with his father so as not to work but to be together in a foreign country that never happened

such is the cemetery he visits each year to think in front of the stone

It is to be forever swimming as best he can between two hands of liar poker. If he responds? Lies. Not respond: kill the truth. The lie, wherein lies the truth. It is the obligation to make believe. It is unavoidable. He submits. Such is the betrayal in order not to betray.

It is the language he speaks, the only one, the one he must speak and that does not belong to him.

It is the untranslatable that remains his dwelling place, uninhabitable, it is the word dwelling [*demeure*] that prophesies in his mouth the minute he says it two always die [*deux . . . meure*]. And yet one must go on living. It is France that has no place except as figure a ghostly country, a spectrality but that he imagines so he can get some rest there between one voyage and the next. A ghostly repose. It is fatigue, it is the dream of one day touching something like land with the tips of his fingers, feet, lips, not only a tallith, flesh, duration, and, yes, the peace of a belief,

And yet one must continue to get lost and dream of believing what one does not believe, a waking dream of what could be, here, if—

I feel lost without French he says, that's something, at least he feels something, which doesn't mean he finds himself in French except in all these figures of cases in point, but at least he renews and increases its powers. He loses his head over French.

So where to find oneself? Will he ever find himself? Where? Save in prison.

In prison? What next? Another illusion? It is this solitude that dogs him, so trusty, so far away so close

In prison outside

Alone with himself

(This would be the place to open the Prison book that gives onto liberty, Prison, where freedom is. It occupies two whole pages, this infinite book, look for it in period 54. A real prison after the series of prisons by proxy.)

It is this noncontemporaneity with all others he has this noncontemporary relationship. With himself. He is not together with himself. It is this *divorce*—the word comes to him in his *Tourner autour des mots*—that he pronounces with himself. He addresses himself as a familiar and tells himself: you are with me and I am not with you.

It is from this mêlée, from this porridge of bloods and songs and ignorance he has salvaged it this incredible language, abducted it, with which, on the edge of which, at the bottom, at the end, at the tip of which, he gets carried away in a flamboyant elevation, trailing a wake of blood. One sees him fly up high high in the sky straight up almost standing on the air, he's a little off kilter I say. Are you leaning to one side? I say me Klein. It's my soul that seems to be dragging a wing says he, Gross. My angelic psyche with its damaged wing.

He flaps one wing.

What are you doing, I shout, the two of you up there, you and your soul?

My life and I are becoming outside he says, we are so high up I don't know if I can translate us exactly.

And where do you think two outsiders [*deux hors*] can come down? he asks.

—Only on a mountain always on the mountain I say, I think, don't you think?

—I think so he says. I'm going to have to stop talking [*se taire*] he telephones me. Pass me an expression for land [*terre*] he say, his *je* being *tu*.

God, I say, I'm giving you God. On a mountain I say, on the mountain.

I have said it from the start the first time I saw him it was in a vision in 1963, a creature, person, figure, animal, "god"—grant me the expression— as he said on the threshold of *Donner la mort* and I grant him the expression, I grant him the "god" that I could see leaping and bounding on the uninter- rupted crest of a mountain, a mountain or perhaps a very high desert, very end without end, an animal neither prodigious nor colossal, but graceful, a primitive vision derived from the first lines ever read. In those days I said a mountain, it was my first apocalypse and there was no name for it. By antono- masia I called him native of the peaks.

Now that I've been posted for a few weeks on the tip of the word *Jew,* I have come to see for the first time that the most ancient characters in my mythological imagination also first manifested themselves on a mountain top, from the peak of their solitude. Of their incredible solitude. I think of the two Separates, who initiated me into a profound and tormented relation- ship with the Bible. Separated by belief. At belief. I think of Moses, the sub- lime doubter, the one who goes out and does not enter. The sentence says: You shall not enter. I think of Abraham, the sublime undoubter. The one who sees the threat in the promise. The sentence says: You shall take. All three of them, beings of the mountain tops, places without reach, crests devoid of sides pure elevation where the word speaks but does not show its face. A crea- ture of the peaks I say, absolutely distant from the cemetery he dreads, he who, if only he knew, is elected for the cemeteryless peaks. All by himself. We need a witness.

How many times have I reread the Bible in order to follow them, by dint of following them. And by dint of not understanding and not understanding, and asking how and why in the end I fell silent and accepted the unaccept- able. For everything that is beyond us filters through the secrets of the writ- ing, his ellipses, his asyndetons, his lightning juxtapositions, there is no bridge, the dictionary from the language of God or rather God-the-sentence (he speaks brief in sentences) to the language of mortals has never existed. But one must read all of Genesis on one's knees on his stones in order to get close to this Abraham of SayingNothing. God says. Done. One must approach him by means of the writing cutting across the means of the writing. As the heart's philosophers, from Kierkegaard to Jacques Derrida, have made us feel, there is an unshareable secret here. But one can sense its waves and tremble with them. I now recognize the path, the sharp stones, the lightness of the air. It is the same mountain, Nebo, Sinai, or the other that I saw in 1963.

He is the divided, the one who—it took me so long to fathom this mystery—strikes the mountain *twice* yes, yes, twice, the one who makes the heart of belief tremble, the philosophical divider, the one who knows that one cannot say I believe without doubting, without crossing out *I* and *believe* and *doubt*.

He is the man in secret, in mourning his smile damp with tears. Condemned—elected—mohel of his soul. In both cases suffering, cruelty. Wrestling with the angel of himself. Jacques on a superhuman scale. Vanquished and vanquisher.

# NOTES

*Translator's note:* English translations of "Circumfession" are taken, with slight modifications, from the version by Geoffrey Bennington (Chicago: University of Chicago Press, 1992). For a more detailed study of Derridan homophones and plays on words, I refer readers to the excellent glossary at the beginning of Alan Bass's translation of *The Post Card*.

I am grateful to Hélène Cixous and Eric Prenowitz for their reading of the translation in progress, and for their clarifications and suggestions.

## AUTHOR'S NOTE

**unorthodox . . . unCatholic** *pas catholique* means, literally, not Catholic, but also, by extension, unorthodox. See also chapter 4 (vii).

**juif, juive** here and later Cixous plays on the distinction, in French, between a male and a female Jew, between the noun *Jew* and the adjective *Jewish* (vii).

**{*sein*} . . . *seing* . . . *saint*** are homophones in French (viii).

**What coif** in French *Quoi faire* (What to do?), in which one also hears *coiffer* (to coif) (ix).

## I. THE MARK OF THE PRINCE

**The Mark of the Prince** the French title, "Le Prince sur le point," puns on the multiple meanings of *point*, including points in an argument, in stitchery (*petit point*), and in punctuation, where a *point* is a period or full stop.

**caginess** *cagité* in French, an invented word, which might also be translated by "caged-ness" (1).

**an I . . . a ni** *un i . . . un ni* (neither) in French, developing into a further homophone, *un nid* (nest) (1).

**dry-witted prince** *un pince-sans-rire* is a dry-witted person (1).

**mocker** *moqueur* in French metamorphoses into *mot-coeur*, "heart-word," and then into *maux du coeur*, "heartaches" (1).

**smiling through tears** is one possible interpretation of the French *sourire* (to smile*) aux larmes*, a phrase derived from *rire aux larmes* (laughing to tears), but which also evokes *fou rire* (mad, unrestrainable laughter) and *sous rire* (under/behind the laughter) (1).

**not possess . . . not have . . . not bear the sight of** the passage plays on the homophony of two French expressions *ne pas l'avoir* and *ne pas la voir* (2).

## II. NAMESAKES—NO! NO'S BY THE BUCKETFUL

**The Call of Names** the French title "L'appel des noms/—Non! Des nons à l'appel" is a complex pun on the homophony of *noms* (names, nouns) and *non* (no), *l'appel* (call, roll call) and *à la pelle* (by the shovelful).

**If I weren't "Jewish"** in French *Si je n'étais pas "juive,"* playing on the distinction, in French, between *juif* and *juive*, male and female, adjective and noun (3).

**J** the sound of the French *J* occurs frequently in this passage, including in the first-person pronoun, *je* (3).

**Jewish . . . story . . . a Jew has a place** in French *une histoire juive . . . une juive trouve sa place* referring specifically to the place of the Jewish woman (4).

**Montagne Sainte Geneviève** in the Latin Quarter of Paris (4).

**indigene/ni/zations** the *ni* inserted here is the *ni* of de*ni*al (4).

**Schools** the most prestigious institutions of higher education in France are the *Grandes Ecoles*, entry to which depends on highly competitive examinations (4).

**back . . . tone . . . gift . . . dose** in French *dos, do, don, dose,* all words that sound the note *do* (5).

**agrégation** the French diploma, based on competitive written and oral examinations, that opens the door to university teaching (5).

*the* **Cir-concision** a play on the word *circumcision* (*circoncision* in French) and *concision* as well as on the gender of this word, which is feminine in French (*la circoncision* . . . she/it) (6).

*apparently* *en apparence* in French can mean in appearance but also outwardly, apparently (6).

**appearance** *apparence* means appearance, semblance, likelihood (6).

**laugh . . . write laughing . . . and that laughing** in French *rire* . . . *Ec-rire* . . . *Et que rire* (7).

**the skein of sons** the French word *fils* means both son and thread (10).

**no-name** plays on the homophony of *non* and *nom* in French (13).

**LI** in French the sounds *el li* (eh-lee) echo throughout this passage like the sounds of the name Elie (13).

**Lit** is a bed in French; *lis* means read; *elle lit,* she reads; *lie* (verb *lier*) means to link or tie; *à la lie* is to the dregs (13).

**escarre** is a bedsore, scar, or a scab; it refers to the sores of the bedridden mother in *Circumfession* as well as to the circumcision scar, and is also a term used in heraldry to designate the L-shaped border of quarter or *équerre*. See also chapter 7 and period 18 for their explorations of related words (14).

**The Elect . . . not to be read** a play on the homophony of *Elie* and *Elu* (elected) and *lu* (past participle of the verb *lire*, to read) (15).

**Elie it is!** in French (*Elie Eh! lis, et lie* . . . ) this paragraph rings with the sounds of the name Elie. See **LI** above (15).

## III. OF KLEINS AND OF GROSSES

**sub*li*me . . . tal*li*th . . . so*li*tary** in French the sound *li* recurs 5 times (17).

**cherished . . . flesh** in French this sentence contains a play on the homophony of *cher* (cherished) and *chair* (flesh) (18).

**starting point . . . nettles him** the French sentence contains a complicated wordplay on *point*, meaning both point of departure (starting point) and no (departure), as well as on the phrase *qui le pique*: that pricks or impresses him and that pinches/steals it from him (19).

*un escarre beau* in period 16. *Escarre* is a feminine noun. See note chapter 2, p. 14 (19).

**s.a.** *société anonyme* (as in inc., incorporated) but also *survivance absolue, Savoir/Savior Absolut*, Saint Augustine, and *sans arrêt* (without end) (20).

**carried away . . . pupil . . . Elysium** the French text plays on *élever* (to raise up, to rear) and on *élève* (pupil) (21).

**A, i** the two letters that pepper period 8 sound like *haïs* (*je haïs*, I hate) but also like *aïe!* an interjection expressing pain or unpleasant surprise (24).

**oto** meaning the ear but in which one also hears *auto* (24).

**God the name dwells in his name** that is, the sounds of the word *Dieu* (God) can be found in Derrida (24).

***Di eu dit du d'yeux*** a sounding out of *Dieu* (24).

***Ni* *that does not deny*** in French *ni* means neither, not and the verb to deny is *nier* (26).

## IV. THE DREAM OF NAÏVETÉ

**Geof** as in Geoffrey Bennington, author of *Derridabase*, the text that appeared with *Circumfession*, which "undertook to describe . . . if not the totality of of J.D.'s thought, then at least the general system of that thought." (*Derridabase*, p.1) (29).

**reads . . . bed** French puns on *lit* (read) and *lit* (bed) (29).

**lets herself be called** in French this section plays on the different senses of *(s')appeler* (to call and to be called or named) (30).

**seven** in French seven is *sept*, pronounced "set," which sound or set of letters can be found in the name Esther (*sept, cet, cette, set, sceptres, accepte, inceste, intercepte*), making for complex wordplay throughout this passage. *J'accepte* (I accept) sounds like *Jacques sept* (Jacques seven), a Derridan signature. There are seven letters in both of Derrida's names (31).

**in every city** in French *à toute cité et cité*, playing on the homonymy of *cité* (city, large town) and *cité* (cited, quoted) (32).

**for his great . . . listen to him** in French this phrase conceals four *pours*: *pour sa plus grande chance dont il ne **pourra** jouir **pourtant** qu'en français **pourvu** qu'on veuille l'écouter* (33).

**Each of us . . . the other** in French *Chacun, sort de l'autre* in which *sort* may be a noun (note the importance of the comma for this reading) or a verb (34).

**mother . . . ocean** in French *la mère* and *le mer* are homophones (34).

**not Catholic** *see* "Author's Note" (vii).

**I am . . . I follow** in French *Je suis . . . je les suis,* playing on the homonymy of *suis* (from the verbs *être* and *suivre*) (35).

**the right to quote** a play on the expression *le droit de cité* (the keys/freedom of the city/ of the cited/quoted) (35).

*I got nothing* in French *je n'eus (rien)*, which to the ear is *Je nu* or *I nude* (36).

**the legacy of her milk** in French *legs* and *lait* (legacy and milk) are homophones (37).

**the legend** or *légende*, in which one hears the sound of *lait* again (37).

**overbidding** in French *surenchère,* in which one hears *chair* (flesh) (38).

**cruelty** in French *cru-el/le* contains *cru* (crude, raw) as well as the feminine pronoun *elle* and the masculine pronoun *le* (39).

**ear/eye** in French a coined word *l'oroeil* (39).

**running after himself** in French this passage plays on similarities in the words *cure, courir, secourir* (40).

**forewarned** the French verb here is *prévenir*, literally, "to come before" (40).

*to fan out your cards* in French *filer (les cartes)*, an expression that means to spread out and arrange one's cards; *filer*, by itself, means, among other things, to spin, to shadow someone, to slip away (41).

*qualis illa erat* such a person was she (42).

*the fastest gun* in English in the original (44).

**what a word** in French *quel mot crusé* after *mot croisé* or crossword (44).

**watch out for it, go after it** in French *le chercher* (search for it), *la chercher* (from the expression *chercher querelle),* to look for a fight (44).

**Marranos** (a term of abuse) is the Spanish word for the Jews in Spain and Portugal who escaped persecution in the fourteenth century by converting to Christianity. Many Marranos, however, continued to practice Judaism in secret. During the Inquisition they were tortured and/or put to death for their beliefs; after 1492, in Spain, and 1497, in Portugal, the Marranos emigrated to North Africa, to other western European countries, such as England and Holland, and to the Americas (44).

**the flesh and ups the stakes to belief** in French *la chair et sa surenchère la croyance,* playing on the sound of *chair* and the different meanings of *cru* (45).

**at the heart of all believing** in French the text plays on the sounds of the words, here *coeur* (heart) echoed by *croire* (to believe) (45).

**raw belief** in French *le tout cru*, which can mean the completely raw, the totally believed, or, modeled on the expression *tout fait*, ready-made belief (46).

**another vein . . . stroke of luck** the French expression *avoir de la veine* means to be lucky; the text at this point is playing on the different meanings of the word *veine* (vein) in French, some of them emphasized and set off by the use of commas (46).

**ear canal** the French *canal* can be translated as either canal or channel: canal seems appropriate for its physiological associations but channel is also apt as a means of communication (46)

**the avowal always vouches . . . blindness** in French the word *aveu* (avowal) is contained in the word *aveugle* (blind) (48).

## V. REMAIN/THE CHILD THAT I AM

***Est-ce taire?*** (*is it to silence ?*) sounds like the name Esther as it is pronounced in French (52).

**homonymy: the child *that I am*** in French *l'enfant que je suis* says both *the child that I am* (verb *être*) and *the child that I follow* (verb *suivre*) (53).

***rev-{ver}*** i.e., in French *ver* is a worm (54).

**dying . . . die . . . mother** in French *mourir . . . meure . . . mère*, words whose alliterations and assonances are lost in English (54).

**to the bottom of this book** *Circumfession* appeared underneath a text by Geoffrey Bennington; it occupied the bottom third of each page (55).

**on the edge of the mother** in French *mer* (sea, ocean) is a homophone of *mère* (mother); their homophony is played on in the following pages (55).

**my emphasis** author's emphasis (55).

**after thirty years** the French *après trente ans* can be interpreted as referring to the writer's age and/or to a period of thirty years. The square brackets here and in the rest of this chapter are the author's (60).

***pied-noir*** name given to French settlers of European extraction in North Africa, and particularly in pre-independence Algeria (60).

## VI. POINT OF HONOR

The French title is "Point Donneur," literally point/no donor but, to the ear, *point d'honneur*, point of honor. The subtitle, *Où il n'y point d'oeil/deuil*, is a play on the homophony of *d'oeil* (of the eye) and *deuil* (mourning).

**my emphasis** author's emphasis (64).

**no point in writing** in French *ne point écrire* suggests both the point in an argument and the point as punctuation, that is the dot, period or full stop at the end of a sentence; hence *ne point écrire* means both stop writing and make no points (64).

## VII. CIRCUMfiCTIONS OF A CIRCUMCISION OBJECTOR

**without his seeing it** the French *à son invu* is a play on the expression *à son insu*, substituting *vu* (from the verb *voir*, to see) for *su* (from the verb *savoir*, to know) (67).

*escarre* see note chapter 2, page 14 (71).

**I have cut myself** the French *je me coupe* can mean I have given myself away, let the cat out of the bag (72).

**alliance** has a broader range of meaning in French, including the wedding ring, marriage and the biblical convenant (72).

**make up your mind** the French verb here is *trancher*, literally to cut or slice (73).

**the *né*** in French *le né* (as in *nouveau-né*, newborn) and *le nez* (nose) are homophones (73).

**"cas de figure"** means both a case in point and one hypothetical solution to a problem. This passage also plays on the different meanings of *figure*: figure of speech, trope, and face (77).

**Each time the son recalls him** in French *Chaque fois que le fils se rappelle*, with an emphasis on the reflexive *se*, so that the phrase suggests *each time the son recalls (himself)* (82).

*Circumcision returns* ... *Schibboleth*, chapter 1 (82).

*vicem, vez* see *Schibboleth,* chapter 1, "We shall find ourselves returning more than once to the vicissitudes of latinity, to the Spanish "vez," to the whole syntax of *vicem, vice, vices, vicibus, vicissim, in vicem, vice vers*a, and even *vicarious*, to its turns, returns, replacements, and supplantings, voltes and revolutions." (82).

**thou-roof** from the French *nés pour n'avoir d'autre toit que toi la langue* which plays on the homonymy of *toit* (roof) and *toi* (you/thou) (83).

**Ev-rejski** I am grateful to Sanja for pointing this wordplay out to me [author's note] (84).

**The going-awayness alliance** in French *La s'en alliance*, which makes *s'en allance*, a phrase coined from *s'en aller* (to go away) and *alliance* (a wedding band and symbol of alliance) overlap and merge (85).

**outside myself and wild about it** in French *hors de moi* which means, literally, outside myself, and, figuratively, wild, frantic, driven to distraction (85).

**marre . . . Marranos** in French *en avoir marre* means to be fed up. For Marranos, see note chapter 4, page 44 (85).


## VIII. THE ORCHARD AND THE FISHERY

The title and the text of this chapter play on the homophony of *pécher* (to sin), *pêcher* (to fish), and *pêcher* (peach tree). La Pêcherie is the name of the Algiers fishing harbor and its neighborhood, a popular meeting place.

**Let's laugh . . . way** this sentence contains a play on *se marrer*, *marre*, and *marri*, echoing the previous chapter's play on *marron* and *marrane* (89).

**fellah** is a peasant in an Arab county (92).

**throws himself off the track . . . slip** French plays on the homophony of *semer* (to sow seed) and *s'aimer* (to love oneself), as well as on other meanings of *semer*, including the figurative *semer quelqu'un*, to shake off (93).

**Un petit ruban** is a reference to a theft that marked Rousseau and that is recounted in *Les Confessions* (93).

**They are too green, says he, good only for goys** *Ils sont trop verts, dit-il, et bons pour des goujats"* (95).

**the 13th comes back** *"La Treizième revient . . . C'est encor la première;/Et c'est toujours la seule";* see "Artemis," by Gérard de Nerval (99).

**Aurelia** from the novel *Aurélia*, by Nerval (99).

**that runs through our texts** *qui faufile nos* textes, literally that bastes or tacks our texts together, but in which we also hear *faux* (false) and *filer* (to spin, to thread, to slip into, to slip away etc.) (104).

**flowerbeds** or *plates-bandes* in French, a compound word with *plates* (flat) and all the senses of *bandes/bander* (106).

**in every color** *sous toutes les couleurs* also evokes the colors of flags or allegiances (107).

*lieutenant* literally the one who is keeping or holding (*tenant*) the place (*lieu*) (107).

**stolen or flitting around** the French, *volé ou volant*, plays on the homonymy of *voler* (to steal) and *voler* (to fly); other words containing *vol* can also be found, *volontiers*, for example (108).

## IX. SECOND SKIN

**Cruel . . . wings . . . Elie** this sentence plays on the sounds of *cruelles, elles, ailes* (wings), and *Elie* (117).

**pass me an expression . . . grant me the expression . . . I grant him** this passage plays on different meanings of the French word *passer* (122).

**cemeteryless peaks** in French *la cime sans tiers*, which contains a play on the word *cimetiere* broken down into *cime* (peak, crest) and *tiers* (third party) (122).

**scale** *échelle*, which also means ladder (123).

# WORKS CITED

## BY JACQUES DERRIDA

*L'Origine de la géométrie*, by Edmund Husserl. Translated with an introduction. Paris: Presses Universitaires de France, 1962; trans. John P. Leavey Jr. Brighton: Harvester, 1978.

*Glas.* Paris:Galilée,1974; *Glas,* trans. John P. Leavey Jr. and Richard Rand. Lincoln: University of Nebraska Press, 1986.

*La Carte Postale. De Socrate à Freud et au-delà.* Paris: Aubier-Flammarion, 1980; *The Post Card,* trans. Alan Bass. Chicago: University of Chicago Press, 1987.

*Schibboleth: pour Paul Celan.* Paris: Galilée, 1986; earlier version, in English, in G. Hartman and S. Budick, eds., *Midrash and Literature*, pp. 307–47. New Haven: Yale University Press, 1986.

"Circonfession." *Jacques Derrida.* Collaboration with Geoffrey Bennington. Paris: Seuil, 1991; *Jacques Derrida.* Trans. Geoffrey Bennington. Chicago: University of Chicago Press, 1992.

"Questions au judaïsme." Interview with Elisabeth Weber. Paris: Desclée de Brouwer, 1996, pp. 73–104.

*Le Monolinguisme de l'autre.* Paris: Galilée, 1996; *Monolingualism of the Other.* Trans. Patrick Mensah. Stanford: Stanford University Press, 1998.

"Foi et Savoir." *La Religion.* Paris: Seuil, 1996.

"La Contre-allée." With Catherine Malabou. *La Quinzaine littéraire/Louis Vuitton*, Paris, 1999.

*Tourner les mots. Au bord d'un film.* With Safaa Fathy. Paris: Galilée, 1999.

*Donner la mort.* Paris: Galilée, 1999; earlier version, in English, *The Gift of Death.* Trans. David Wills. Chicago: University of Chicago Press, 1996.

"H.C. pour la vie, c'est à dire," in *Hélène Cixous, croisées d'une oeuvre.* Paris: Galilée, 2000.

"Un Ver à soie." *Voiles.* Paris: Galilée, 1998; *Veils.* Trans. Geoffrey Bennington. Stanford: Stanford University Press, 2001.


### OTHER WORKS

Celan, Paul. *Gespräch im Gebirg. Gesammelte Werke,* 3:169 ff. Frankfurt: Zuhrkampf, 1983; *Selected Poems and Prose of Paul Celan.* Trans. John Felstiner. New York: Norton, 2001.

Rousseau, Jean-Jacques. *Les Confessions.* Paris: Gallimard, 1995.

Montaigne. *Journal de voyage en Italie. Oeuvres complètes.* Paris: Gallimard, 1962.

Beaumarchais. *La Folle Journée* ou *Le Mariage de Figaro.* Paris: Livre de Poche, 1989.

*European Perspectives*

❖ ❖ ❖ ❖ ❖ ❖ ❖ ❖ ❖

A SERIES IN SOCIAL THOUGHT AND CULTURAL CRITICISM

Lawrence D. Kritzman, editor

European Perspectives presents outstanding books by leading European thinkers. With both classic and contemporary works, the series aims to shape the major intellectual controversies of our day and to facilitate the tasks of historical understanding.

Julia Kristeva *Strangers to Ourselves*

Theodor W. Adorno *Notes to Literature*, vols. 1 and 2

Richard Wolin, editor *The Heidegger Controversy*

Antonio Gramsci *Prison Notebooks,* vols. 1 and 2

Jacques LeGoff *History and Memory*

Alain Finkielkraut *Remembering in Vain: The Klaus Barbie Trial and Crimes Against Humanity*

Julia Kristeva *Nations Without Nationalism*

Pierre Bourdieu *The Field of Cultural Production*

Pierre Vidal-Naquet *Assassins of Memory: Essays on the Denial of the Holocaust*

Hugo Ball *Critique of the German Intelligentsia*

Gilles Deleuze and Félix Guattari *What Is Philosophy?*

Karl Heinz Bohrer *Suddenness: On the Moment of Aesthetic Appearance*

Julia Kristeva *Time and Sense*

Alain Finkielkraut *The Defeat of the Mind*

Julia Kristeva *New Maladies of the Soul*

Elisabeth Badinter *XY: On Masculine Identity*

Karl Löwith *Martin Heidegger and European Nihilism*

Gilles Deleuze *Negotiations, 1972–1990*

Pierre Vidal-Naquet *The Jews: History, Memory, and the Present*

Norbert Elias *The Germans*

Louis Althusser *Writings on Psychoanalysis: Freud and Lacan*

Elisabeth Roudinesco *Jacques Lacan: His Life and Work*

Ross Guberman *Julia Kristeva Interviews*

Kelly Oliver *The Portable Kristeva*

Pierra Nora *Realms of Memory: The Construction of the French Past*

vol. 1: *Conflicts and Divisions*

vol. 2: *Traditions*

vol. 3: *Symbols*

Claudine Fabre-Vassas *The Singular Beast: Jews, Christians, and the Pig*

Paul Ricoeur *Critique and Conviction: Conversations with François Azouvi and Marc de Launay*

Theodor W. Adorno *Critical Models: Interventions and Catchwords*

Alain Corbin *Village Bells: Sound and Meaning in the Nineteenth-Century French Countryside*

Zygmunt Bauman *Globalization: The Human Consequences*

Emmanuel Levinas *Entre Nous*

Jean-Louis Flandrin and Massimo Montanari *Food: A Culinary History*

Alain Finkielkraut *In the Name of Humanity: Reflections on the Twentieth Century*

Julia Kristeva *The Sense and Non-Sense of Revolt: The Powers and Limits of Psychoanalysis*

Régis Debray *Transmitting Culture*

Sylviane Agacinski *The Politics of the Sexes*

Alain Corbin *The Life of an Unknown: The Rediscovered World of a Clog Maker in Nineteenth-Century France*

Michel Pastoureau *The Devil's Cloth: A History of Stripes and Striped Fabric*

Julia Kristeva *Hannah Arendt*

Carlo Ginzburg *Wooden Eyes: Nine Reflections on Distance*

Elisabeth Roudinesco *Why Psychoanalysis?*

Alain Cabantous *Blasphemy: Impious Speech in the West from the Seventeenth to the Nineteenth Century*

Julia Kristeva *Melanie Klein*

Julia Kristeva *Intimate Revolt and The Future of Revolt: The Powers and Limits of Psychoanalysis*, vol. 2

Claudia Benthien *Skin: On the Cultural Border Between Self and the World*

Sylviane Agacinski *Time Passing: Modernity and Nostalgia*